The Detroit Tigers

◆

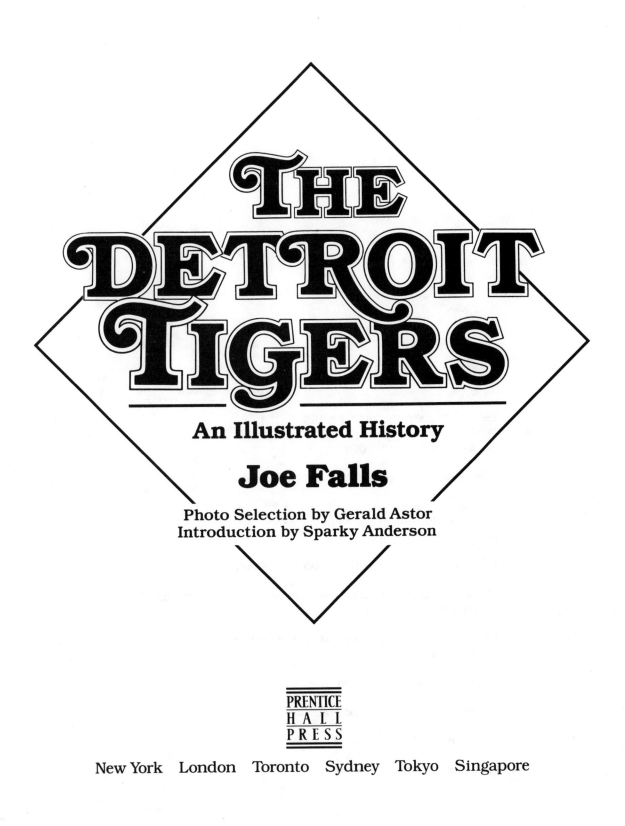

THE DETROIT TIGERS

An Illustrated History

Joe Falls

Photo Selection by Gerald Astor
Introduction by Sparky Anderson

PRENTICE
HALL
PRESS

New York   London   Toronto   Sydney   Tokyo   Singapore

PRENTICE HALL PRESS
15 Columbus Circle
New York, NY 10023

Copyright © 1989 by Joe Falls and Gerald Astor

Published by arrangement with Walker & Company.

PRENTICE HALL PRESS and colophon are registered trademarks
of Simon & Schuster, Inc.

Library of Congress Catalog Card Number: 89-63600
ISBN 0-13-202698-8

Designed by Joyce C. Weston

Manufactured in the United States of America

10   9   8   7   6   5   4   3   2   1

First Prentice Hall Press Edition

CREDITS AND
ACKNOWLEDGMENTS

♦

p. 1 (opp.), 2 (top), 3, 4 (bot.), 5, 6, 8 (top), 9, 11, 13, 16, 20 (bot.), 21, 23 (top & bot. rgt.), 24, 25 (bot.), 29, 30 (rgt.), 33 (bot.), 35, 38, 39, 40, 41, 42, 43 (top & bot. rgt.), 45, 49, 53 (bot.), 54, 57, 58, 60, 62, 63, 65 (rgt.), 69, 70, 71 (bot.), 73, 74, 78, 79, 83 (top), 86, 87, 88, 91 (top), 99, 100 (bot.), 103 (bot.), 106, 128 (top rgt.), 132, 133 (bot.), 134, 135, 136, 139, 144, 162, 163, 164, 167, 174 (bot.), 183, 185 (bot.)
Detroit *News*

p. 2 (top), 22, 26, 27 (top), 28 (bot.), 37 (top lft.), 52, 53 (top), 80, 81, 90, 91 (bot.), 92 (rgt.), 98, 114, 120 (lft.), 126, 128 (bot.), 138, 151, 153 (lft.), 155, 166
Burton Historical Collection, Detroit Public Library

p. 4 (top), 7, 18, 20 (top), 23 (bot. lft.), 25 (top), 27 (bot.), 28 (top), 30 (lft. & ctr.), 32, 33 (top), 37 (top rgt. & bot.), 44, 46, 47, 50, 56, 61, 65 (lft.), 71 (top), 72, 75, 76, 82, 83 (bot.), 92 (lft.), 93, 95 (rgt.), 96, 97, 100 (top), 103 (top), 108, 109, 111 (bot.), 113, 115, 120 (rgt.), 122, 124 (bot.), 125, 127, 128 (top lft.), 129, 130 (top lft. & bot.), 131, 148, 149, 153 (rgt.), 156, 157, 176 (bot.)
National Baseball Hall of Fame Library

p. 8 (bot.), 12 (top & bot.), 14, 94, 118, 124 (top), 166, 178, 179
Detroit Tigers

p. 43 (ctr.), 68, 84, 95 (lft.), 102, 111 (top), 116, 117, 122, 146, 150, 158, 160, 171, 172, 174 (top), 177, 180, 181, 184, 185 (top & ctr.), 186
Bettmann UPI

p. 66, 137, 142 (bot.), 176 (top)
Wide World

p. 130 (top rgt.), 142 (top)
Detroit *Free Press*

p. 133 (top)
Herb Scharfman, *Sports Illustrated*

Ty Cobb by Charles Alexander. 1984. Reprinted by permission of Oxford University Press, New York, N.Y.

To M.J.
for all the soft boilers
and hugs

CONTENTS

◆

INTRODUCTION

◆

I've been in Detroit for ten years now, which is longer than I was at Cincinnati. That's special to me. A lot of things are said about this city, but let me tell you this: I can't think of a better place to make your living if you happen to be in this game of baseball. You never get bored around here. Something is always going on. And don't ever kid yourself: these people know their baseball.

They've torn me a new hide. They can be very tough but they're also very fair. If they've got a gripe, they'll let you know about it. But if they think you're doing your job, they'll let you know that, too.

They care about their baseball team, and when you get right down to it, that's the most important thing of all.

Detroit has been a great baseball town all through this century. I'm looking forward to reading this book, because I don't know all the things I'd like to know about Ty Cobb and Harry Heilmann and Mickey Cochrane and Hank Greenberg and Charlie Gehringer. Those are great names. They are names that live with us until this day.

I'll tell you this: if I could manage the guys in this book, I'd be around forever. Jim Campbell would have to open the vault and give me a lifetime contract. Just think of the batting order you could put together:

Charlie Gehringer, 2B   Mickey Cochrane, C
George Kell, 3B   Al Kaline, RF
Ty Cobb, CF   Alan Trammell, SS
Hank Greenberg, 1B   Hal Newhouser, P
Harry Heilmann, LF

I would have John Hiller and Willie Hernandez down in the

bullpen, and if Wahoo Sam Crawford had nothing to do with his time, he could be my DH.

We have some great traditions in baseball: New York, Boston, Chicago, Philadelphia, Cleveland, Pittsburgh, Cincinnati, St. Louis. The old cities. The ones which have been around forever. Detroit is right up there with them. When you think of Detroit, one of the first things you think of is the Tigers.

I remember when I walked into Briggs Stadium back in the 50's and looked around at all those green seats, I thought I never saw a more beautiful place in my life. It was like we were inside an old cathedral. I found myself whispering.

It is called Tiger Stadium today, and the seats are blue, but you still get the shivers when you look around this ballpark. You can almost see the ghosts out there. I think of what it was like when Hughie Jennings was the manager. I try to imagine those days, but I can't quite make it. So it's good somebody wrote this book about the history of baseball in Detroit.

I've got a special name for Joe Falls. I call him "Old 75." That's because he is good to me 75 percent of the time he writes about me. Somebody told me about the chapter he did on me. I think I'm going to have to start calling him "Old 95."

Maybe I should put Ty Cobb up first because if he got on base 300 times a year . . .

SPARKY ANDERSON

The Detroit Tigers

◆

OUR HOMETOWN TEAM

◆

I t was different in the old days. You'd walk into our ball-park and smell the aroma of those hot dogs on the grill. We have some of the greatest hot dogs in America. Jim Campbell, president of the Tigers, is proud of his hot dogs. "Six to a pound," he'll tell you. "Nobody else gives you six to a pound." And they plump as you cook them, just like it says on TV.

Well . . .

Now they've gone ahead and added sausages—with peppers and onions. That's what you smell these days. The sausages, peppers, and onions overpower the aroma of the hot dogs, but it's hard to get mad about it because a sausage in a bun, covered with peppers and onions, wrapped in a sheet of waxed paper, is not the worst thing in the world to eat during a ball game. After all, we must understand these are modern times.

We had a lovely ballpark in the old days. People used to come to Detroit and swoon over our ballpark. It felt so comfortable. It felt like ballparks were supposed to feel. Our seats used to be green. The grass was green. The walls were green. Even the roof was green.

If you were from Philadelphia, you felt at home in Detroit because our ballpark made you think of Shibe Park. The same if you were from Washington, Boston, Pittsburgh, Cincinnati, St. Louis, Chicago, or New York. We had a little from the old world for you here in Detroit.

For some reason, they changed our ballpark. They tried to turn it into a stadium. Didn't they know there was a difference between a ballpark and a stadium? Ebbets Field in Brooklyn was a ballpark. Three Rivers in Pittsburgh is a stadium. One is a pair of slippers, the other a pair of new shoes.

Traffic struggles for a single lane through the downtown streets as citizens hail the win over the San Diego Padres in the 1984 Series. ◆

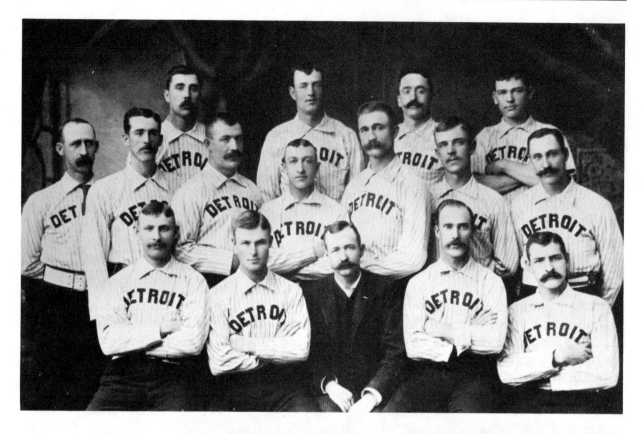

The 1887 championship team. ♦

A capacity crowd packs Navin Field in 1931 although the Great Depression had already seized America. ♦

Somebody got the idea—I think it was those politicians downtown—that our ballpark ought to look like Yankee Stadium. They ripped out the green seats and put in blue ones. They also put in some orange seats. Pretty soon our ballpark looked like a Howard Johnson's restaurant.

They told us they couldn't get green seats. They said plastic wouldn't reproduce in green.

A call to the manufacturer in Grand Rapids produced the following response: "I can make any color green they want—pea green, sea green, soup green, emerald green, forest green. You name it, they can have it. But hey, man, I've got an order for 50,000 blue seats. Don't screw it up on me, will you?"

Okay. We don't like the blue seats, and the orange seats look absurd, but the grass is still green and it is still 325 feet to right and 340 to left and the flagpole stands tall and proud in center field. We can live with the changes because we love our ballpark. Just because she is wearing some strange eye makeup doesn't mean we can't give her a hug.

Some people laugh at us. They poke all kinds of fun at Detroit. We're right up there with Buffalo and Cleveland on the joke list. Maybe we've even taken over the top spot. Ever see a travel poster inviting you to visit Detroit on vacation?

We shoot each other and we burn buildings and we've got drug dens that are among the worst in the land. It is not safe to walk around some neighborhoods, and not only have we closed up some of our factories (farewell, Dodge Main), but we're now

Concessionaires whooped it up in the bleachers before the start of a 1935 World Series game, when hot dogs sold for a dime and a bag of peanuts went for fifteen cents. ◆

4

The 1907 American League pennant-winning squad. ◆

Navin Field became Briggs Stadium in the mid-1930s and Tiger Stadium in 1961. The lights installed in 1948 give some of the best illumination in the majors. ◆

Some Detroiters cele-
brated the 1935 World
Series victory by festoon-
ing the town's most fa-
mous product. ◆

closing up some of our churches. We're still embarrassed about
that terrible scene after the final game of the 1984 World Series.
That was the night we burned the police car outside the ballpark
and danced around the flames.

That's us. Detroit. Big, bold, bawdy Detroit. But we're not
that bad. We give more money to charity than any city you can
name. We've got great hospitals and a marvelous university—
Wayne State—in the heart of town. Our symphony struggles,
but when it's got its act together, it can play with the best of
them. We've got a splendid bridge to Canada, a sparkling water-
front, wonderful tree-shaded streets, and in Greektown, the most
marvelous lamb chops you could ever hope to find. And nobody,
anywhere, makes meat sauce like Aldo's at the corner of Moross
and Kelly. To dine at Aldo's late on a wintry Sunday afternoon,
when the week's work is done and all is mellow, is to make a
brief visit to heaven.

When you get right down to it, though, the best things we
have are our baseball team and our ballpark.

That's because we've had them for so long and they are special
to us. They treat us well.

Have you ever hugged a ballpark? You ought to try it. It's fun.
We did it a year ago when there was talk around town about
tearing the place down and putting up one of those domed sta-

In the 1890s the future site of Navin Field was a dusty crossroads bounded by Michigan, Trumbull, and National Avenues. The first rickety wooden stands were built in 1901 to seat 8,500. ♦

diums. A lot of people got upset. They didn't know what to do, so they got together and made a ring around the ballpark. They joined hands and gave the old place a big hug. I'm told a few even kissed the walls.

Don't ask me to explain all of this. I'm just an outsider. A transplanted New Yorker who has lived here only thirty-six years. I grew up with Ebbets Field, the Polo Grounds, and Yankee Stadium. Now I sit in the press box at Tiger Stadium, where it is warm and dry and the hot dogs and Cokes are free. We are more than a hundred feet from the field and watch the game through windows. What can any of us know up there? But if you walk around enough and talk to enough people, you can get a feeling they truly do love this ballpark.

More than any other structure in the city, the people of Detroit relate to Tiger Stadium. They all know where it is, what it looks like, and what it feels like. Tiger Stadium—formerly Bennett Park, Navin Field, and Briggs Stadium—has become an enduring symbol of Detroit.

We used to have a great department store on Woodward Avenue in downtown Detroit. It was called J. L. Hudson's. You could take the kids there to look at the toys at Christmastime. Gone.

We used to have this massive red brick building on Gratiot Avenue where the Stroh Brewery made that wonderful beer. It was a mighty fortress, standing against the sky—and how marvelous it was to see white smoke curling into the winter sky on those icy mornings when you drove into town. Gone.

We had a giant stove out on East Jefferson, near the Belle Isle Bridge. I never knew what the stove meant but you could not help but look at it and smile every time you drove past it. Gone.

The General Motors building still stands in midtown Detroit, just as the famed "Glass House"—headquarters of the Ford Motor Company—stands in Dearborn. Lee Iacocca, the boss of Chrysler, still keeps his office in Highland Park, which is really part of Detroit. All these buildings are Johnny-come-latelies, however, compared to our ballpark. Besides, you can't smell sausages, peppers, and onions when you walk into their lobbies.

Sam Greene, Harry Bullion, H. G. Salsinger, Edgar Hayes, Lyall Smith, Bud Shaver, Malcolm Bingay, and Bob Murphy. Forgive me. This is personal. These are some of the old Detroit sportswriters, the ones who went before us and showed us the way to the clubhouse, the dugout, and the batting cage. These are my heroes, the men whose words and experiences are recalled in this book under the name of this transplanted New Yorker.

Our ball club (see how easy it is to become provincial?) has been with us through almost all of this century. It got us through those early years when Henry Ford was trying to convince us that it was better to sit down in a moving machine than to climb onto a horse in order to get around town. Our team has brought us happiness and sadness. It gave us a reason to cry and a reason to laugh. It gave us a reason to feel proud. It brought us diversion, and that's very important in this hardworking town.

The Tigers took us through two World Wars—and even if the games looked a little strange during the 1940s, we loved them

Bennett Field housed the Detroit entry as the American League established itself in 1901. Along with the permanent seats running down the first and third baselines, spectators stood behind ropes in the outfield for big games. The field was put down over a cobblestone surface dating from the time the site served as a hay market. The grass failed to cover all of the cobblestones, making for frequent bad bounces. ♦

On chilly spring and fall days during the 1930s, ticket sellers bundled up in overcoats and hats warmed themselves with portable electric heaters. ◆

Mickey Cochrane's 1934 American League pennant winners. ◆

anyway. Who remembers Prince Oana, the right-hander from Waipahu, Hawaii, who was three-and-two in 1944 and smacked that line drive homer against the Yankees that never got more than 20 feet off the ground before it crashed into the center field seats? We needed the Tigers in those days. When we had no jobs during the Depression or when the days in the war plants grew long and tiresome, at least there was something to talk about. If you couldn't afford the trolley fare and a ticket to the game, Ty Tyson would bring you all the action on WWJ radio. Too bad you could never see the beret he wore.

The Tigers were there for us after the riot of 1967. It would be foolish to say they cooled off the city in the spring of 1968, but they gave us something else to think about. They were winning games in the seventh, eighth, and ninth innings. This was exciting in itself, and it let us know that there was still some sanity in this violent world of ours.

John F. Kennedy had been shot in Dallas. Martin Luther King was gunned down while standing on the balcony of his motel in Memphis. Robert Kennedy was struck by an assassin's bullet and died on the kitchen floor of a Los Angeles hotel. Who could understand these things? Who could cope with them? There was unrest on our campuses—death by gunfire. The streets of

Straw hats, caps, placards, and flags decorated the standees in the outfield during the first decade of the twentieth century. Early ground rules awarded three bases for balls hit into the crowds. Later it was reduced to two. ◆

Watts, Newark, and Detroit burned. We were burdened with Vietnam, a war that wasn't a war. We had flower children strolling among us and many were popping pills and shooting drugs as they cried out for freedom and peace.

At least there was one place where the world was unchanged. It was still 90 feet between the bases and the home team wore that Olde English *D* on the front of their uniforms and most of the games were played at 1:30 in the afternoon. We had something we could hold on to—a place where we could feel secure. Three strikes and you were out, and four balls and you were on first base, and hardly anyone called balks.

Happily, they brought us "The Bird" in 1976. He made us forget the rising interest rates and falling economy. Japan was making better cars than we were and gas would go to two dollars a gallon and you had to wait an hour or more to get to the pumps.

Mark Fidrych would talk to the ball—"Stay down, ball. Stay down. Stay low, ball."—and this gave us some momentary relief. The Tigers won for us again in 1984, came close in 1987, and, perhaps most amazing of all, finished just one game out in 1988 with a lineup that looked like something out of Double-A ball. Chet Lemon batting cleanup?

Nowhere else is the daily drama in Detroit played out more clearly than at the ballpark. Who hasn't stood in the batter's box with Darrell Evans as he narrows his eyes and sets his sights on the pitcher? Who hasn't come skipping in from shortstop with Alan Trammell to take that two-bouncer on the short hop and fling it over to first base? We're not sure how the tight end of the Lions got free in the end zone, or how the puck got through that maze of players in front of the Red Wings' net, but we all can see Lou Whitaker going into the hole for that hard grounder, Dave Bergman making a backhand stop of the ball near the bag at first, or Matt Nokes grinding his hands on the bat as he waits for the next pitch.

There is no hiding on the ball field. The most wonderful thing about it all is that when the game's over, the team'll come back and do it again the next day. They might even get it right. If they don't win this season, maybe they'll do it next season. All they need is another right-handed hitter and a little help in the bull pen. Right?

If the Tigers are eternal, we are eternal. You think Tom Brookens looks any different than George Kell did when he played third base? They both hunch over and set themselves in a locked position as the ball is about to be delivered. Look at them closely. They're both a little bowlegged. We don't remember Ty Cobb except from the pictures, but how much different could he have

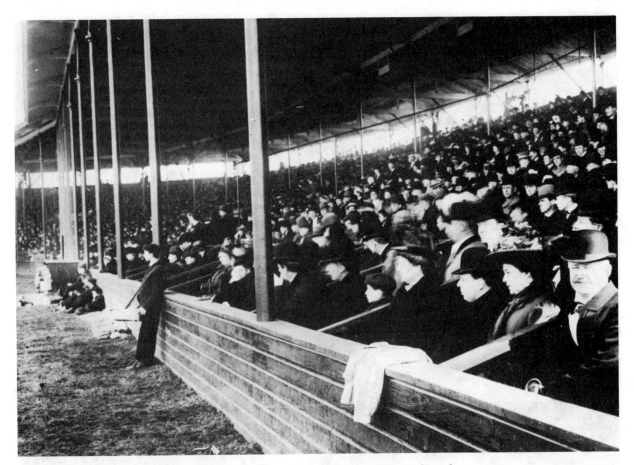

been from Kirk Gibson? Gibby was no Cobb at the plate, but he was mean and he was intense and he would barrel into you if it meant getting an extra base. We had George Mullin on the mound in the early 1900s, but was he any different than Jack Morris? Who can tell the difference between the way Hughie Jennings ran the club and the way Sparky Anderson runs the club? Both are colorful characters. Besides both like to talk.

Our team is important to us because it reminds us of our heritage. It links us with this entire century. When Pete Rose was chasing his 4192nd hit a few years ago, it brought us back to the time when Ty Cobb was compiling his great record for the Tigers. You could almost see the fans' straw hats and watch them drink their lemonade in the grandstand section of Navin Field.

You think today's Thunderbird looks like yesterday's Model T? Not even close. Our cars have changed as much as time itself. Whatever became of running boards, anyway?

But baseball is pretty much the same now as it was a hundred years ago. Things certainly haven't changed much on the corner of Michigan and Trumbull, except the trolley tracks are gone.

Most of the paying customers at Bennett Park in the early 1900s sported derbies, but women were already among the devotees. ◆

The 1945 World Champions. ♦

The come-from-behind
1968 champs. ♦

We park our cars in the same places—in lots and gas stations, on front lawns and backyards. We go through the same turnstiles, and if the scorecards are a little different, the pencils are the same. If we're lucky, we sit in the same seats. The posts don't even bother us anymore. So what if you can't see all of the second baseman? He doesn't make that many plays, anyway.

We can all relate to the Tigers because who hasn't played a game of ball at some point in his life? They've made us mad and they've made us glad. At times they've infuriated us so much that we've clicked off our TV sets and promised to do more worthwhile things, such as taking the dog for a walk. Or maybe taking a nap.

But we always go back. We are drawn to the ballpark by an invisible force. We wonder what's going on, and if we're not there, we turn on the radio and listen to Ernie and Paul. We may stay with them for only a moment, maybe half an inning. But we wait until they give us the score. You never turn off Ernie Harwell or Paul Carey until you get the score.

We all know how the Tigers made out the night before. The word is everywhere—on the radio, on TV, in the newspapers, on trains, planes, and buses; in schoolrooms, restaurants, courtrooms, offices, factories, gas stations—even behind the drawn drapes of hotel rooms. Everyone knows how they did the night

Groundskeepers tend the playing field in 1931 when the American League still had clubs in Philadelphia and Washington. ◆

before. Maybe all they get is the score. Maybe that's all they want. "Hey, they lost again, 5–4! What's the matter with those guys?" You don't even have to call them by name when you're complaining about the Tigers. Who else would lose 5–4?

Some people are into it very deeply. Not only do they know the runs, hits, and errors from the night before, but they've picked up on the fact that Alan Trammell moved up two inches in the batter's box in order to reach Roger Clemens' fastball. It's best to listen politely to these people and move on as quickly as possible. Otherwise they'll be asking you what kind of vegetables Charlie Gehringer grew on his family farm in 1922.

This may be a weakness on our part. We should probably have more important things on our minds. We can't help ourselves. We're not opera people, and you've got to drive forty miles to find a good music theater. We like to bowl, if you must know it, and we put mustard, onions, and chili on our Coney Island hot dogs. We don't have a very grand downtown sector and it isn't wise to walk around it after dark. But we do have the Tigers, and they stir us in many ways. How can you not react to Gary Pettis popping up—not again!—with two out and the bases loaded?

More people probably know about Sparky Anderson than they do Coleman Young. Coleman Young is merely the mayor of Detroit. People get mad at him, but not the way they get mad at Sparky. The mayor doesn't have to decide whether to leave Jack

The 1984 World Series victors. ◆

S C R A P B O O K

"Beneath the cover of news-center choppers and gray skies, nearly 1,000 Detroiters locked hands and embraced their ancient ballpark at 6:03 last evening before the Red Sox–Tigers game was rained out. It looked like the world's largest police line.

"We're not talking serious civil disobedience here. As demonstrations go, this fell short of the Chicago Seven and the Catonsville Nine. It was beautiful.

"They hugged the facade that abuts Kaline Drive and curled around to the side that outlines Cochrane Avenue. A couple of lucky huggers embraced the plaque outside the main entrance which reads: 'Registered Historic Site . . . The evolution of this stadium is a tribute to Detroit's support of professional athletics.'

"Tiger Stadium is Michigan Registered Historical Site No. 470."

Detroit News, 1988

◆

"[Ernie Harwell] is a broadcasting institution. He has been behind a mike 48 years now, 40 in the majors. He was the first active member of his profession to be inducted into the Hall of Fame and, at 70, is still going strong. . . .

"Harwell and his partner of 16 years, Paul Carey, do all 162 on radio. All 162 every year. Harwell has missed just one game in his nearly three decades with the Tigers.

"'August '68,' he said. 'It was my brother's fault. He died, and I had to go to his funeral.'"

Bob Rubin, *Inside Sports*, 1988

◆

"Frank Navin had finally given up on further enlargements to Bennett Park and decided to build a completely new facility, on the same site but re-oriented so that homeplate would be where left field had been. Undertaken as soon as the 1911 season was over, demolition of the old park and construction of the new one went forward smoothly through the fall and winter, so that by March, the all steel-and-concrete stands were almost finished. The Tigers would open their home season in a park that cost half a million dollars and had seats for about 23,000 people. With covered, single-decked grandstands, covered pavilions, bleachers in right field, and a green concrete wall (kept free of advertisements) in left, it was an attractive and commodious place, a first-class home for the Detroit ball club. Its features included dressing rooms for both home team and visitors, in accordance with Ban Johnson's [American League president] edict that starting in 1912 all visiting teams must dress on the grounds rather than at their hotels. At Yawkey's insistence, the new park was named Navin Field."

Charles Alexander, *Ty Cobb*

◆

Enthusiastic young Tiger fans promise the franchise will remain healthy for the future despite the relatively small size of the metropolitan district. ♦

Morris in there or bring in Willie—excuse me, Guillermo—Hernandez from the bullpen.

Right from the start, the Tigers commanded our attention. The team has always had more than its share of star players. In the beginning, it was Ty Cobb—and what a wondrous player he was—a man of immense skills. If anyone hits .367 these days, he is set for life. Cobb hit .367 over a twenty-four-year career. When Cobb left the scene, there was the impeccable Charlie Gehringer to carry on. When Gehringer started slowing down, Hank Greenberg came along. He was a man of powerful presence—a tremendous home run hitter and the first great Jewish athlete in Detroit. When Greenberg was gone, sold unceremoniously to Pittsburgh, there was Al Kaline, smooth, smart, and sleek, to hold the torch for twenty-two years. If Cobb wasn't around, you wouldn't find a better player than "Wahoo" Sam Crawford, and did you you know that Harry Heilmann—Old Slug—batted .342 in his career? He spent thirty-four years with the Tigers—seventeen on the field and seventeen in the broadcast booth. To this day people miss him on the air. It seems as if the Tigers have always had somebody standing on center stage. Mark Fidrych had the spotlight for only one year, but what a year it was. The girls of Detroit sent him enough birthday cakes in 1976 to last him a lifetime. Denny McLain played a starring role for four years, winning thirty-one games in 1968, and breaking rules and records with equal abandon. Now it's Trammell, Morris, Whitaker, and Nokes.

For nearly all of this century, the Tigers have been there for us. We rode horse and buggies to see them, then trolley cars, then automobiles. Sometimes we walked, especially when they played during the daytime. When they started their games at 3:30 P.M., we had time to get there from our factories and our schools.

They can paint our ballparks blue and orange, and they can give us young ushers in their neatly tailored uniforms, and hand out caps and cups and balls and bats as we go through the turnstiles. All that is fine. But when we show up, we show up for one reason only: to see a ball game. It makes us feel good.

THE "EE-YAH" YEARS

♦

T hey asked Davy Jones, the old outfielder of the Tigers, for the secret of his success.

"Easy," said Jones. "I have myself a limburger sandwich and two bottles of beer before I go to bed."

Times were simpler when the Tigers—or the Detroits—or the Creams—were getting started in the city of Detroit. Baseball did not begin in Detroit with Ty Cobb's emergence from the red clay hills of Georgia. It only seems that way. He was the one who brought attention to Detroit in the early 1900s, but the origins of baseball in this city stretch back into the 1870s, with the first organized team playing in 1881. In fact, the mayor himself, the Honorable W. G. Thompson, was responsible for founding the first team. He was the team's first president, and the club's mail address was the mayor's office.

The population of Detroit was slightly under 120,000 in those days, and nobody had heard of Henry Ford or his Model T. The club was called "the Detroits," in contrast to the singular "Chicago," "Boston," or "Providence." The games were played at Recreation Park on the east side near the intersection of Brush and Brady Streets.

TV? Radio? Lights? Artificial turf? Long-term contracts? The players were lucky if they got a clean change of underwear once a week.

Baseball was a crude operation in those days. The players didn't receive any meal money—though once in a while the owner, in a fit of charity, might hand them twenty-five cents apiece and tell them to go out and have themselves some pigs' knuckles and cold beer for dinner.

The playing fields were grubby. They were bumpy, and almost

Hughie Jennings not only managed, he also coached third. Here he demonstrates his coaching dance step and encouraging shout of "Ee-yah!" ♦

Davy Jones was the third and lesser man in the outfield beside Crawford and Cobb. ♦

The Detroit professional teams played at rickety Recreation Park during the 19th century. ♦

devoid of grass. The bases weren't anchored and would fly around when runners slid into them. The clubhouses were little more than run-down shanties. The players knew nothing of whirlpool baths, electrotherapy, skilled trainers—or even hot water. They would wait in line and take turns for the single cold shower, using yesterday's towel to dry today's body.

Their uniforms were often damp and smelly. "Sometimes they'd be out-and-out wet when we put them on," said Ty Cobb. "They were jammed into containers after a game in their natural sweat-soaked state, and that's how we would find them the next day. We'd put them on again even though they were a grimy disgrace. They seldom saw a laundry, but nobody said anything because that's the way it was with all of the teams."

The pitchers were allowed to doctor the balls with any substance they liked in those days. They applied coats of talcum, slippery elm, licorice, or just plain spit. They nicked the balls with their fingernails and little was said by the umpires. The players did not enjoy such luxuries as padded walls, cinder tracks, or sunglasses. If you slammed into the fence and got hurt, it was your own fault. But you'd better not leave the game, because there was always somebody else to take your place. You bandaged your own wounds and carried on.

An early problem for the owners of the Tigers were the "wildcat bleachers" beyond the left field fence. The fence ran along an alley behind a row of houses on National Avenue. The property

owners out there soon realized that their backyards afforded a bird's-eye view of the game. They built rickety stands on their property and charged fifteen cents to sit in them. These outlaw seats attracted an unsavory element that constantly caused trouble in the neighborhood. Gambling and fistfights were rampant. The regular fans were subjected to verbal abuse as they walked through the alley on their way inside the ballpark. The police tried to control these bullies, but could never quite do it. They would restrain them one day, but the wildcats would be back the next.

From time to time, the management of the Tigers put up strips of canvas to obstruct the view from these bandit bleachers, but this only caused more trouble. The fans sitting out there hurled obscenities, as well as vegetables, at the players, and soon the obstruction came down so the games could go on.

The two most popular players on the first team in Detroit were catcher Charlie Bennett and center fielder Ned Hanlon. Hanlon was the captain of the "Detroits." In those days, the captain ran the team on the field while the manager tended to business in the front office.

In 1887 Detroit held a franchise in the National League and finished at the top of the heap. At bottom right is catcher Charlie Bennett, for whom the field was named. Outfielder Ned Hanlon, the mustachioed gent, back row—second from right—later managed the Baltimore Orioles. He owned ten percent of that club while holding an equal share of Brooklyn, in an era when a number of proprietors maintained such divided loyalties. Dan Brouthers, third from left middle row, was a slugging first baseman and is in the Hall of Fame. ◆

The "Detroits" lasted eight years in the National League, from 1881 to 1888. Bennett and Hanlon played all eight years and became very close friends. They often went on hunting trips together. On such a trip in 1894, Bennett suffered a tragic accident. According to Fred Lieb's early history of the Tigers, the two men were on a train bound for Kansas City when it made a brief stop in a small Kansas town where Bennett stepped off to speak to a friend. As he attempted to reboard, he lost his balance and fell under the train's wheels. He was taken to a hospital, where his left foot was amputated at the ankle and his right leg at the knee. Bennett had made his home in Detroit when he first started playing with the team in 1881 and he continued to live there after his terrible accident. He opened a cigar store to support himself. He was the first catcher to wear a chest protector on the outside of his uniform, and the fans were so taken by his skills that the first ball yard in Detroit was named in his honor— Bennett Park.

Another near-tragedy struck the Detroit club when William H. (Wattie) Watkins, one of the first managers, was struck in the head by a pitched ball in a game in Bay City, Michigan. He escaped with his life, but his hair turned white.

In those days, the players were a rowdy crew. According to *The Spalding Guide* in 1889: "The two great obstacles in the way of success of the majority of professional ball players are wine and women. The saloon and brothels are the evils of the baseball world at the present day; and we see it practically exemplified in the failure of noted players to play up to the stan-

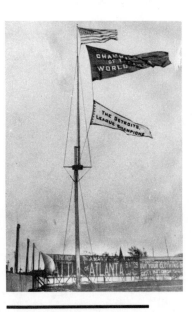

Bennett Park, seen here on opening day 1901, was the smallest of the major league arenas by the time Ty Cobb arrived in 1905. It seated only 8,500. There was only one shabby dressing room for the hometown club and visitors dressed in their hotel rooms. ♦

Recreation Park hoisted Old Glory and then flew the world and league championship flags captured by Detroit in 1887. ♦

By 1917, when this photo was taken, the Georgia Peach seemed more content with his teammates and his manager Hughie Jennings. He called Jennings "a wonder" who broke up the cliques of the club and through adroit diplomacy brought Tiger dissension to an end. Jennings assigned feuding players to share bathrooms in hotels or sleep in opposite Pullman berths, forcing them to accept one another. Jennings was regarded by some Tigers as being too lenient with Cobb. ♦

The view from right field at old Bennett Park. ♦

dards they are capable of were they to avoid these gross evils. We tell you gentlemen of the National League, the sooner you introduce the prohibition plank in your contracts, the sooner you will get rid of the costly evil of drunkenness and dissipation among your players."

Ty Cobb was never one to abuse his body. He did occasionally chase after women, but he maintained a strict regime of eating and sleeping habits, believing this gave him an edge over his competitors. In fact, he was such a stickler for physical conditioning that he did not like to eat too soon after the games, because he was so wound up from the competition. He felt it would be easier to digest his food if he rested for several hours. So after each game, he'd return to his hotel, buy a newspaper, stretch out in bed, and read for a while. Sometimes he'd sit by the window and look out, or take a little nap. He was always careful to preserve his strength where possible. Only after he rested would he sit down to dinner.

Somehow, word of Cobb's strict regime got out during the 1908 World Series against the Chicago Cubs. The fans in Chicago picked up on it and gathered in the streets outside of the Lexington Hotel, where the Detroit team was staying, and made noise all through the night. Cobb was livid. He summoned manager Hughie Jennings to his room and demanded that Jennings do something about the mob in the streets.

"Ty, what can I do?" said Jennings. "It's out of my hands."

"You're the manager," said Cobb. "Think of something."

Cobb claimed he did not get to sleep until 4 A.M. the next morning. Jennings told him: "I didn't sleep at all."

Cobb spat back: "But you're not playing."

On April 28, 1896, a new ballpark was christened in Detroit at the corner of Michigan and Trumbull—present site of Tiger Stadium—Bennett Park! Old Charlie Bennett hobbled to the plate on crutches and caught the ceremonial first pitch thrown by pitcher Jack Fifield.

The Park was inaugurated with a game against the Columbus team. In the bottom of the first inning, the Columbus center fielder was chasing a long fly off the bat of George Stallings when he collided with a spectator crossing the field. The two men lay stunned in the outfield while Stallings circled the bases for a home run. Fifield, the pitcher, helped his own cause with two home runs though he was thrown out at the plate on the second one after the Columbus third baseman tripped him. The rules were rather loose in the early years of baseball.

At one point, the Detroit team was known as the "Creams." That name showed up in print in 1894. How they became the Tigers has been a subject of debate for nearly a century. Initially, baseball historians credited Phillip J. Reid, city editor of the *Detroit News*, with first using the name "Tigers" in print in 1896. Manager George Stallings had put black and brown stockings on his players, and the hose reminded the fans of tiger stripes.

George Stallings guided the Tigers in 1901 to third place in the American league, not yet recognized by the National League as its equal. Later Stallings took the Boston Braves to a National League pennant and World Series title in 1914. ◆

The very first action photo taken at Bennett Park shows New York Highlander third baseman Wid Conroy leaping for a throw under the eyes of the Tiger coach and Umpire Silk O'Laughlin. ◆

Catcher Deacon Jim McGuire broke in with Toledo in 1884, did a turn with Detroit as a National League entry in 1885, returned to the Motor City in 1902–1903 and, at age forty-seven, played one more game for the Tigers in 1912. ◆

But on April 16, 1895, the *Detroit Free Press* printed a headline that read: "Stallings' Tigers Show Up Very Nicely." On the same page, a string of baseball notes appeared under the heading: "Notes of the Detroit Tigers in 1895." Curiously, the name "Tigers" did not appear in either story, but from then on, the name was accepted by the public.

For a time in the 1890s, Detroit had a team in the International Association, and for a while it had no team at all. The big breakthrough came when Ban Johnson, the Cincinnati sports editor, accepted Detroit's application to join the new Western League, which he hoped to build into another "major league." The owner of this Detroit team was James D. Burns, the Wayne County sheriff, who was also a prosperous hotel owner. His first manager was Stallings, who later went on to manage the "Miracle Braves" in 1914. Nobody knew if there was enough interest in Detroit to sustain a team. The old Detroits had been forced to disband because of a lack of interest. The new team played its first American League game on April 25, 1901. The ballpark was set up for 6,000 patrons, but a stunning 10,013 people showed up and overran the place.

Detroit's first lineup showed Jim (Doc) Casey at third base, Jim Barrett in center field, Bill (Kid) Gleason (later the manager of the infamous Chicago Black Sox) at second base, Bill (Ducky) Holmes in right field, Frank Dillon at first base, Norman (Kid) Elberfield at shortstop, Bill Nance in left field, Fred Buelow catching, and Roscoe Miller and Emil Frisk pitching.

Most of the fans made their way to the game by buggy or on bicycle. The rest walked. The overflow crowd was placed behind ropes in the outfield. Milwaukee provided the opposition and took an early 7–0 lead, which became 13–4 by the ninth inning. Many of the fans left, disgusted with the performance of the hometown team. But the Tigers started to rally in the bottom of the ninth. Casey led off with a double and Barrett singled him home. Holmes and Dillon both doubled. The rally continued, and when Dillon came to bat again, the Tigers were trailing 13–12 with three men on and two outs. The fans who'd stayed in the park were going crazy at the comeback. Dillon responded by smacking his fourth double of the day, driving the ball into the outfield crowd and giving the Tigers a 14–13 victory. Baseball was in Detroit to stay.

The city was just beginning an economic revolution that few understood at the time. Not many people put faith in the new horseless carriages, which were beginning to creak through the streets of Detroit. They wondered about the odd-looking man in Dearborn who was turning out those strange machines.

Defenders of Detroit Baseball Prestige in 1903. In those days, with the American League in its third year, the Tigers played their home games in Bennett Park, later to be Navin Field. The styles pictured were then the height of fashion, and Bill Donovan, second from the left, in the back row, was considered a Beau Brummel. From the left, back row: Rube Kisinger, pitcher; Donovan, pitcher; Sam Crawford, outfielder; Charley Carr, first base; Jack Deering, pitcher; Billy Lush, outfielder; Fritz Buelow, catcher. Front row: Lee Henry, secretary and treasurer; George Mullin, pitcher; Mal Eason, pitcher; Doc Gessler, outfielder; Frank Kitson, pitcher; Jack Lilley, catcher; Jimmie Barrett, outfielder; George Smith, second base; E. G. Barrow, manager. ◆

Bobby Lowe was over the hill when he closed out his career at Detroit, 1905–1907. But in the depths of the Dead Ball Era, before manufacturers increased resilience in baseballs, Lowe in 1894 became one of a handful of players to smack four homers in a single game. ◆

Henry Ford's idea of a power-driven automobile would prove to be a tremendous boon to the city. Workers from all over the middle west and Canada converged on Detroit, seeking jobs in Ford's auto plants. Likewise, immigrants heard of the opportunities in Detroit and they, too, flocked to the city. Almost overnight the population began to grow, and attendance at the ballpark downtown grew with it.

Bennett Park was not the ideal place to play baseball. The field was set up at the site of the old Haymarket, which had originally been paved with cobblestones. When they built the field, only a few inches of loam were spread over the cobblestones. This gave the field an uneven surface, and balls often took weird bounces. Fielders always had an alibi for their errors. When they'd muff one, they'd simply say: "It hit another cobble."

Ed Barrow, listed as manager for Detroit in this 1905 illustration, actually quit during the 1904 campaign. Bobby Lowe, the second baseman, served as field manager for the remainder of 1904 until Bill Armour took command for 1905. Sam Crawford, the slugging outfielder, was the star until August of 1905 when a nineteen-year-old Georgian, Tyrus Raymond Cobb, arrived on the scene. In this era teams limited themselves to rosters of 18 with four or five pitchers. ♦

Bill Coughlin was the Tiger third baseman from 1904 to 1908. ♦

When Ty Cobb showed up, the groundskeepers adjusted the field to suit his talents. They kept the area in front of home plate soaked to slow down his bunts, while making it more difficult for the fielders to pick up the balls.

The quagmire soon became known as "Cobb's Lake." When Cobb became the manager and a hard-hitting team came to town, he would have the grounds crew set up temporary bleachers to turn long drives into ground rule doubles. Detroit was proving to be an imaginative addition to the major league scene.

In 1902, Sam Angus, an insurance man, purchased the club and appointed an owlish, poker-faced man named Frank Navin as his bookkeeper. Navin would become the guiding force behind the Tigers for the next three and a half decades. Angus's bankroll was soon depleted, and Navin scouted around for a new owner—someone with money, but also someone who would allow him to keep running the club. He was in the process of completing a deal with lumber baron William Clyman Yawkey, who was the richest man in Michigan at the time, when Yawkey suddenly died. Yawkey left $10 million to his son, William Hoover Yawkey, who was only 28, so Navin started courting him. He convinced Yawkey that the Tigers would be a sound investment. The younger Yawkey bought the club for $50,000 and gave Navin $5,000 in stock. The Tigers were on their way as an established franchise in the American League.

Young Yawkey was a playboy and traveled extensively. Baseball didn't interest him very much. He turned over the entire operation to Navin, who ran it as if it were his own property.

Yawkey would occasionally drop by to watch his team play. He liked to pal around with the players. He trusted Navin implicitly.

Surprisingly enough, Yawkey was a shrewd businessman with a quick mind, who built his fortune from $10 million to $40 million. Once, on a trip to Chicago, Yawkey invited two of his players—Germany Schaefer and Charlie O'Leary—to have breakfast with him at the Congress Hotel. The players ordered ham and eggs, and a glass of milk each. When Yawkey saw that the milk cost ten cents a glass, he jumped to his feet and said, "This is an outrage! I can buy a whole quart of milk for that money!" He summoned the bellboy to his table, gave him a dollar, and told him to go out and buy a quart of milk. The boy returned with the milk and put ninety cents change on the table. Beaming with delight, Yawkey told the lad to keep the change, and poured the milk for his two players. (Yawkey's son, William Yawkey, Jr., later owned the Boston Red Sox.)

While it was Ty Cobb who created the excitement, it was another man—the scholarly Hughie Jennings—who brought stability to the Detroit franchise as its first great manager. For one thing, Jennings knew how to handle Cobb. He gave Cobb the freedom he needed to develop his own spectacular skills. This was one of the wisest moves ever made in the Tigers' history, because Cobb became the greatest player in the game. And besides, he wouldn't have listened to anyone anyway.

Starting in 1907, Jennings managed the Tigers for fourteen seasons—still the longest tenure on record. He won pennants in his first three years—'07, '08, and '09. He was a happy man, a blue-eyed, freckle-faced Irishman with a fine sense of humor, who always seemed to have a smile on his face. Even Cobb's demands never brought him down. Jennings was the most colorful manager of his day, and the fans of Detroit came to love him.

He was the son of a Pennyslvania coal miner, and started working in the mines as a young boy for ninety cents a day. It was his job to fan the mules to keep the flies off them as they

The shrewd Frank Navin guided the team from 1902 until his death in 1935. He took over complete ownership of the Tigers from William Yawkey following the 1909 season. ◆

Jennings hit .312 as a player. His career began with Louisville in the American Association in 1891, and he spent about half of his major league career as a Baltimore Oriole. He managed the Tigers for fourteen years, winning pennants his first three years, 1907–1909. But the Tigers lost all three World Series.

"Hughie Jennings played an excellent shortstop, but at first he was not much of a hitter. The story is that he learned to overcome his habit of stepping away from the pitch by standing with his back to a wall so that he could not pull away and having McGraw throw close to him until he overcame the fault."

Harold Seymour,
Baseball, The Early Years ◆

hauled coal up from the mines. He played semi-pro ball for the staggering sum of five dollars on Saturday afternoons, eventually working his way to Baltimore where he played with those famous Oriole teams of the late 1880s—the Wee Willie Keeler, John McGraw, Wilbert Robinson, and Kid Gleason Orioles.

While playing in Baltimore, Jennings attended Cornell University in the off-season and even though he could barely read or write at the time, he earned a law degree. He was admitted to the bar, worked in his brother's law office, and became known as an excellent trial lawyer. He had a way with words, and the English language became one of the passions of his life. His handwriting was almost perfect.

Jennings' early life taught him the value of the dollar. He saved his money and preached economy to his players, most of whom were a wasteful lot. He invested money in homes in Brooklyn and realized a solid return. He invested in securities and soon became a director of several banks. Through it all he maintained a feeling for the common man.

Jennings often went back to the mining towns in Pennsylvania where he grew up. He would wait outside the mines at the end of the day and offer the tired, sooty workers rides home in his car or groceries for their families. He did this quietly, without any publicity, because he never forgot his origins.

When Jennings played shortstop for the Orioles, he was the team's most aggressive player. His specialty was getting hit by pitched balls to set up rallies. In those days stepping in front of pitches was permissible, and he was hit as many as three times in one game and 49 times in one season. One time, in Philadelphia, he was struck on the head but stayed in the game. Afterwards, he collapsed and was unconscious for three days.

At Cornell, where he coached the baseball team in exchange for his tuition, young Jennings decided to go swimming one evening. It was dusk, and he neglected to turn on the lights in the swimming hall, so he did not know the pool was empty. Jennings dove off the springboard and landed head first on the concrete floor. He was dazed, but otherwise unhurt.

His greatest feat, aside from taking a listless Detroit team to three straight pennants, was simply existing with Cobb. Almost immediately, Jennings saw the brilliance of his young outfielder. He also recognized Cobb's stubborn manner. He took Cobb aside and told him he could play the game at his own speed. "There isn't anything I can teach you about baseball," Jennings told Cobb. "Anything I might say or do will only hinder your development. Do as you please. You have my support. You can teach yourself how to play this game better than anyone else can teach you. Do what you think is necessary and I'll back you up."

Cobb's special treatment didn't sit too well with the other players. Cobb took advantage of his manager sometimes, showing up late for spring training and occasionally not showing up at all. But when he reported, he was always in shape and outplayed everyone else. Nothing could be said—the results spoke for themselves.

At times Cobb would try Jennings's soul. Once, when the team was in Chicago, Cobb complained because his room overlooked a train yard. He said the noise kept him awake. Jennings said there wasn't much he could do about it, and that they were all bothered by the noise. Cobb packed up and returned to Detroit, missing the last two games of the series. Jennings let him get away with it.

Only once in anyone's memory did Jennings discipline his star. Cobb had gotten into a street fight and his manager was so mad at him that he benched him for two games. When Cobb returned after the suspension, he won the game with a triple.

As the years went by, the two men became close friends. Cobb didn't like many people, but he had a genuine affection for his manager. They would sit up at night and go over the games, trying to think of new ways to win.

They were both crowd pleasers in their own ways. Jennings would work the coaching lines and he had the habit of kicking one leg into the air and crying out, "Ee-Yah! Ee-Yah!" At first he was yelling, "Here we are!" but shortened it to "Ee-Yah" as the years went by. The fans loved it, and would pick up on his chant from the moment Jennings took his place in the coaching box. Another favorite cry was "That's the boy!" which he shortened to "Attaboy!" He became as much a public favorite as Cobb.

Jennings gave his signs in simple words. He fooled the opposition entirely. They never dreamed he would do such a thing. They thought he was just a guy who liked to talk a lot. He employed this ruse for all fourteen years in Detroit.

Jennings was among the first to play mind games. He said, "You never waste your time or energy scolding a man in anger. It does no good. When you are angry, your reasoning isn't sound. If you must scold a player, let him know that by taking time with him, you are paying him the highest compliment possible."

Even though the Tigers won three straight pennants under Jennings, they could not take the World Series.

In the club's first appearance in a World Series, the 1907 Tigers met the Tinker [Joe] to Evers [Johnny] to Chance [Frank] Chicago Cubs, who only a year before had won a record 116 games in the regular season. The outfit that faced the Tigers had "slumped" to 107 victories using a five-man pitching staff with an e.r.a. of 1.67. Still, as a team Detroit led both leagues with a .266 average; the Cubs averaged only .250.

In the opening game at Chicago, the Tigers led 3–2 going into the bottom of the ninth. But with a man on third, a ball got by Tigers catcher Charley "Boss" Schmidt. The runner scampered home to tie the game, which was still 3–3 after the twelfth inning. Darkness forced the umpires to call the contest, and it went into the books as a tie.

Boss Schmidt was playing with a broken bone in his hand, and the Cubs exploited him and his substitutes for a total of

The 1907 crew included a trio of Hall of Famers: Sam Crawford, Hughie Jennings, and Ty Cobb. Bill Donovan and Twilight Ed Killian won 25 games each, George Mullin another 20. ♦

18 stolen bases as they swept the next four games with scores of 3–1, 5–1, 6–1, and 2–0. The final whitewash was delivered by Mordecai Centennial (he was born on July 4, 1876) "Three Finger" (his pitching hand was mangled in a farm machinery accident while he was a boy) Brown.

Ty Cobb had batted only .200 in the Series, compared to his .350 during the season; Sam Crawford, a .323 hitter, managed only .238 in the Series. Poor Schmidt took such a ribbing from fans over his poor play—a broken hand was an insufficient excuse—that he was placed under a doctor's care after the Series ended.

The World Series of 1908 rematched the two teams. The Cubs were coming off another incredible season; they had beaten out New York after the famous boner by Giants rookie Fred Merkle, who failed to touch second on a hit ostensibly scoring the winning run in a late-season game between Chicago and New York. Instead of a Giant win and a Cub loss, it was a tie. Chicago then recovered to beat out New York. Chicago had managed 99 wins in the season; the pitching staff's e.r.a was 2.14, and the club hit .249. Detroit's pennant came with a mere 90 wins, an e.r.a. of 2.40, and with Cobb, the team's leading hitter, batting a mere .324. Sam Crawford was second at .311.

Hoping to cash in on the rematch, owner Frank Navin erected temporary bleachers in the outfield and hung huge sheets of canvas behind them to block the view from the makeshift seats constructed beyond the confines of the field. But only 11,000

Sam Crawford from Wahoo, Nebraska, still holds the career record for triples with 312. An outfielder, he played the last fifteen years of his nineteen-year career with the Tigers, starting in 1903. ◆

The local heroes, including pitchers George Mullin, Bill Donovan, and Edgar Willet, ride in triumph after the 1908 pennant win. They dropped the Series to the Chicago Cubs 4–1. ◆

paid their way in for Game 1. The faithful seemed on the verge of being rewarded as the team broke on top. Cobb starred with a single in the first to drive in the initial run; another single in the seventh eventually enabled him to score on an infield out. In the eighth he reached first when Chance dropped the throw on a bunt, and then came home on a bad throw from the outfield on another hit. When the Cubs came in for their last licks at the top of the ninth inning, they trailed by a run. But six straight singles by Chicago turned a 6–5 Tiger win into a 10–6 loss.

In Game 2, a scoreless tie ended in the eighth with a six-run Cub rally. Cobb's ninth inning home run brought in the only tally for Detroit. Game 3 was a Cobb extravaganza; he had three singles and a double. By the ninth inning when he was on first, he felt confident enough to wage a typical Cobb terror campaign. He loudly announced his intention to steal second and when he did, he knocked Joe Tinker on his backside. Cobb then yelled that he intended to take third and he slid in under catcher Johnny Kling's throw. The next hitter, Claude Rossman, was walked and, in a maneuver favored by Cobb and the Tigers, he rounded first and trotted toward second. Usually catchers would throw to second and Cobb would dash for home. But Cub pitcher Ed Reulbach cut off the throw and fired to third, where Harry Steinbach tagged Cobb. No matter, however: Detroit won its first World Series game, 8–3.

The glory died the next afternoon. The nemesis of 1907, Three Finger Brown, shut out the Detroiters 3–0, and not only did Cobb go hitless, but Brown fielded Cobb's attempted sacrifice bunt and forced a runner at third. Game 5 was equally dismal, as Orval Overall blanked the Tigers 2–0, and Cobb again went without a hit. The last game drew only 6,210, and the losing players' shares were worth just $871 per man. The owners, in a rare fit of generosity, gave each player an extra $145 from the Series gate receipts.

After the Series, Cobb was dubbed "the Georgia Peach" by W. A. Phelan in an article in *The Sporting Life*. Phelan wrote: "He is not a lemon but a peach."

When the team earned its third straight shot at a World Series in 1909, at least the Chicago Cubs were not present to torment them. Although Frank Chance had led his team to 104 wins, the Pittsburgh Pirates had topped them with 110 victories. The encounter was spiced by the confrontation between the Pirates' genial hitting and fielding marvel, shortstop Honus Wagner, and the irascible batting phenomenon Ty Cobb, who had won the AL home run title with 9. Promoters brought them together to pose for the new-fangled moving picture camera and the pair

chatted amicably about their techniques with a bat for the silent film.

Game 1 realized the hopes of the 30,000 on hand. Cobb, on first after a fielder's choice, broke for second. The throw was low and to the bag, but Cobb's hook slide carried him safely beyond the reach of Wagner's sweeping glove. But the Tigers' hopes ended when a long fly by Cobb in the seventh with two on was snagged by Pirate outfielder Tommy Leach and Pittsburgh won the contest 4–1.

Cobb broke open Game 2 when he stole home in the third inning, and the Tigers shot to a 5–2 lead. The final score was 7–2. Game 3 belonged to Wagner with his three hits, three RBIs, and three steals in a Pittsburgh 8–6 win. The Tigers evened matters in Game 4 as Ty knocked in a pair and George Mullin shut out the National Leaguers 5–0. Cobb's temper was not improved, however, since he was thrown out twice on bunts.

Sam Crawford, whose bat had slumbered in the two previous Series, now awakened with a roaring homer, double, and single in Game 5. But it wasn't enough, as Pittsburgh won 8–4. The Tigers revived in Game 6, eking out a 5–4 triumph. Cobb drove in one with a ball that rolled into the overflow crowd for a ground rule two-bagger. However, the victory was painful. Tom Jones,

Honus Wagner of the Pittsburgh Pirates slaps the tag on Detroit's Tom Jones as the Tigers lose the 1909 Series 4–3. ◆

the first sacker, left in the ninth after a collision. Battered Charley Schmidt behind the plate was spiked tagging out a runner, and George Moriarty suffered a similar wound putting the ball on a runner at third to snuff out a Pirate rally.

Pittsburgh's Babe Adams, who had won the first and fifth games, now shut out Detroit in Game 7 for an 8–0 win. Adams had not expected to start the opener, but Howard Camnitz, Pittsburgh's ace, was unable to pitch because of a bout with the bottle. Adams was such a hero in Pittsburgh that many women in the crowd followed him back to his hotel after the final game and refused to leave until he came out and gave them all a kiss.

Detroit, which, led by Cobb, had lived by the stolen base, died by it, as the Pirates swiped 18 bases. The Tigers were now three-time losers in the World Series.

Frank Navin used his share of the receipts from the Series to pay off his final obligations to Bill Yawkey and take over the Tigers, free and clear. Although the Tigers were consistently in the first division, they did not win another pennant for Jennings after the 1909 season and, finally, the entire experience got to him. He started to drink. He became tired of his job.

On October 15, 1920, Jennings resigned as manager and sent the following letter to Navin:

Mr. Frank Navin
Detroit Base Ball [sic] Club

Dear Sir:

I hereby tender my resignation as manager of the Detroit Base Ball Club, to take effect at the expiration date of my contract on Oct. 15, 1920.

I take this step with considerable regret. Our relations from the date of my coming to Detroit, and continuing through all these years, have been most cordial and pleasant. However, I have studied the base ball situation in Detroit and feel a change would be beneficial to you and the Detroit Base Ball Club, and perhaps to myself.

I will watch with a great deal of pleasure the work of your club, and will always be pulling for its success. I am

Yours truly,
Hugh Jennings

Before leaving, Jennings suggested that Cobb take over the managerial reins. Cobb didn't think much of the idea. He was still too wound up in his own performance to take on such a responsibility. Cobb suggested that Navin should hire Kid Glea-

Donie Bush (left) played shortstop on the Tigers during the Cobb era. Said Sam Crawford, "Bush was a superb shortstop, absolutely superb." William "Kid" Gleason (right) filled the second base slot for Detroit in 1901–1902 but achieved fame as manager of the ill-starred Chicago White Sox of 1919 who dumped the World Series. ♦

son away from the White Sox. He was a pepper pot of a man who might wake up the Tigers. Navin, though, wanted Cobb.

Cobb went home at the end of the season and was duck hunting in Louisiana when he ran into E. A. Batchelor, a Detroit sportswriter, who was in New Orleans to cover a football game involving the University of Detroit. They had a drink together, and Batchelor told Cobb that the Tigers needed him as their manager.

"No way," said Cobb. "I don't need that kind of grief."

Batchelor told Cobb that if he didn't take it, the job would go to Pants Rowland, who had managed the White Sox from 1915–1918.

Cobb had never liked Rowland. He thought it had been a fluke when he won the 1917 pennant with Chicago. Cobb felt Rowland was a fraud and that Kid Gleason was really running the team from behind the scenes.

"I could never play for Rowland," spluttered Cobb.

"Well . . ." Batchelor said.

"Okay, okay, I'll consider it," said Cobb.

Cobb became the new manager on December 18, 1920. It was a major story. Writers came in from all over the country for Cobb's official signing. When Damon Runyon congratulated Cobb on his new job and his increase in salary, Cobb glared at him.

"This is anything but a present," he said. "This thing has been forced on me."

The Great Man must have known something. He worked hard at his job. He spent a lot of time with his hitters. He turned Harry Heilmann into one of the most feared batters in the game.

Harry "Heinie" Manush benefitted from coaching by Cobb, who urged him to choke up, cut down on his swing, and hit the ball where it was pitched instead of trying to pull it. Manush became the fourth Tiger outfielder to enter the Hall of Fame, with a lifetime average of .330. In 1928 he was traded to St. Louis for three spear-carriers. ♦

S C R A P B O O K

"There was a whirl of black and yellow stockings and dark uniform. Jennings was coming across the field at a pace I never saw any shortstop equal before or since, and the crowd, a decent crowd and willing to give fair play, was trying to split out and give him room. But they couldn't. They were massed so thickly they could give him hardly space to plunge his head. . . . He dove into the crowd like a football star and seemed for an instant to rise high above their heads. We saw him lift his hands then go down, diving headfirst and vanishing, while his spikes flashed for an instant as he disappeared. And the next second, up he came, holding the ball above his head."

Wee Willie Keeler on a play by Jennings against Chicago, *Detroit News*, 1910

◆

"I never had as many fights as they said. As far as spiking anyone is concerned, I doubt that I deliberately spiked more than one or two players in the entire twenty-four years I was in the big leagues. When I came up to Detroit, I was just a mild-mannered Sunday School boy. Sam Crawford then was the big dog in the meat house and I was just a brash kid. But, as soon as they started to put my picture in the papers and give me some publicity, the old-timers began to work on me.

"They practically put a chip on my shoulder, hazed me unmercifully and every time I'd put down my hat I'd find it twisted into knots on my return. But now that I look back on it, I think that's a better system than the gentlemanly treatment the rookies get these days. If I became a snarling wildcat, they made me one."

Ty Cobb

◆

"Sam [Crawford] was in 154 championship battles this year, and in 76 tussles he delivered blows that netted the Tigers one or more runs. In 47 arguments Crawford drove in two counters, in each of eight passages at arms he drove in three, in one fracas he drove in four, and in one skirmish he drove in five runs. Smiting Sam did most of his demon and timely walloping against the Cleveland pitchers and found the Chicago gunners the most puzzling set of artillerists."

Ernest J. Lanigan, *Detroit Free Press*, 1910

◆

Heilmann's lifetime average of .342 includes four seasons above .390, with a .403 mark in 1923. Heilmann became the voice of the Tigers on radio some years after he hung up his spikes. Ted Lyons, former White Sox pitcher, said, "Harry Heilmann was one of the most marvelous men I ever met in baseball and one of the greatest right-handed hitters. Harry had a choppy stroke, but powerful." ◆

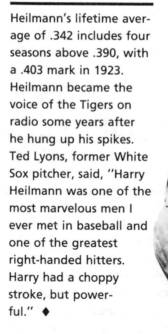

But Cobb could never find the winning touch. As a playing manager, he finished sixth, third, second, third, fourth, and sixth, before moving on to Philadelphia to close out his career with Connie Mack.

Cobb always defended his record as a manager. He would tell anyone who would listen, "In no way do I consider myself a failure as a manager. I took over a seventh-place club in 1921 and, with one exception, all my clubs won more games than they lost. We were in the first division four times. We played interesting and exciting ball. We drew well on the road. Next to the Yankees, we were the best draw in the league."

Yes, but no cigar.

1921: Ty Cobb, now managing the team, kneels far left, second row. Standing back row, third from left, is Harry Heilmann, the heir to Cobb as the town's batting hero. Others on the club include, front row, left to right: Donie Bush, Sammy Hale, Ira Flagstead, Joe Sargent, Coach Tubby Spencer, Coach Bobby Veach; second row: Cobb, Doc Ayers, Lu Blue, Dick Dayton, Ralph Young, Johnny Bassler, Clarence Huber; third row: Bob Jones, Howard Ehmke, Heilmann, Carl Holling, Clyde Manion, Red Oldham, Parrott Livingston. ◆

THE DEMON

♦

The crowd roared as Ty Cobb walked to the plate. How many more times would they get a chance to see the great man take his turn in the batter's box? This was at an old-timer's game in Yankee Stadium. Cobb was sixty years old.

His eyes narrowed as he looked around the field. He wanted to see how they were playing him.

He turned and looked at the catcher. "Maybe you'd better back up a little bit," Cobb said. "I'm not so good at holding the bat anymore. I don't want it to slip out of my hands and hurt you."

The catcher nodded and backed up a few strides. On the first pitch, Cobb laid down a bunt in front of the plate and beat it out for a base hit.

Tyrus Raymond Cobb: Competitor.

They used to have a custom in Detroit on Labor Day. The men would wear their straw hats to the game and the first time the home team did anything at all, they would stand up and scale their hats onto the field. This symbolized the end of summer.

Cobb was managing the Tigers in those days, and told the grounds crew that when the straw hats started sailing out of the stands, they should pick them up as quickly as possible. He told them to store the hats in the equipment room next to the clubhouse.

When the season ended, Cobb loaded these straw hats into his car and drove them back to his home in Augusta, Georgia, where he would place them on the heads of the donkeys working in his fields, shading them from the sun.

Tyrus Raymond Cobb: Character.

Each day after the players left, Cobb would go into the shower

Saving ground, Cobb touches the inside of third, while heading for the plate. ♦

The sunny side of Ty Cobb flashed for a photographer in 1923, but neither opponents nor teammates saw many grins. ♦

room and pick up the small pieces of soap they left on the floor. These, too, would go back to Augusta with him at the end of the season, soap for the hired hands.

Tyrus Raymond Cobb: Curmudgeon.

Some say Cobb was the greatest player of all time. He certainly compiled one of the great records of all time. For twenty-three straight years he batted better than .300. He won twelve batting championships. At one time he held 90 major league records, including the highest career batting average—.367—a mark that stands to this day.

But it was his personality, not his numbers, that made him such a fascinating figure. He was cold, calculating, cunning, crafty, and caustic. He was not a large man—six one and 175 pounds—but he played with an intensity that frightened those around him. He was an all-out competitor who would stop at nothing to beat you. He would think nothing of sinking his spikes into your ankles if he thought you were going to tag him out. He was—in his way—a master showman. He was a man with a massive ego who had to keep inventing new ways to satisfy that ego.

In his final years with the Philadelphia A's, when his great skills were fading away, he put on an exhibition of hitting that stunned the New York Yankees during pregame batting practice one day at Shibe Park.

Urban Shocker, the Yankee pitcher, was kidding Cobb from the bench. "Let's see you hit one to right!" Shocker yelled out.

Cobb lined the ball just inside the first base line.

"Now let's see you hit one into left!"

Cobb smacked a drive just inside the left field foul line.

"Now drop one into center!"

Cobb again obliged, and hit the ball straightaway.

"Let's see you hit one into the dugout!" Shocker cried out.

On the next pitch, Cobb sent a screamer into the Yankee dugout; he followed with another liner that sent Shocker scrambling for safety.

The great man stood there with a smirk on his face.

Cobb was a true craftsman at the plate. He had no set batting stance. He would bat from the front of the batter's box or from the rear. He'd bat off his toes or back on his heels. He did whatever he felt was necessary to give him an edge on the pitcher. If Ty Cobb's life was about anything at all, it was a constant attempt to get an edge on his opposition.

Sometimes Cobb would swing hard and intentionally miss the ball. Then he'd drop down a bunt and catch the third baseman flat-footed and deep. Or he might fake a bunt and, as the fielders came racing in, he'd drill the ball past their ears.

Cobb takes a cut during opening day ceremonies of the Pacific Coast League in the late 1930s. ♦

Posing long after retirement, Cobb showed off the split-handed grip which allowed him great bat control. Late in his career, when he was thought to be in decline, Cobb whacked five homers in two games to demonstrate he could reach the fences. ◆

Ty worked out elaborate schemes of cat-and-mouse with pitchers; he was naturally the cat. He put on plays with hitters that enabled him to take an extra base, running with an intensity never before seen. ◆

When Cobb hit the dirt against the Philadelphia Athletics, his raised right foot slashed the arm of third sacker Frank "Home Run" Baker. Even the soft-spoken Connie Mack, manager of the Athletics, was roused to condemn Cobb as a dirty player. With irate fans threatening his health, Cobb played several games in Philadelphia surrounded by a cordon of cops. ◆

> "Ty Cobb is the hardest man in the league to get. He is fast and he can throw his body like an eel. You can't figure on what side he is coming. It seems as though he can throw his body while he is diving at the base. You make a pass for him on one side and he simply jerks by on the other. I really do not think that Ty ever tried to spike a baseman intentionally. He comes in so fast and throws his body so quickly that he cannot figure on the position of the baseman."
> —Henry Beckendorf, Detroit catcher 1909–1910 ◆

More than once, he stole second, third, and home in the same inning. He did it once on three straight pitches, bragging loudly about his intentions each time. He was a master psychologist, always playing mind games with the opposition.

During one game against Boston, a photographer by the name of Dick Sears was sent to the ballpark with instructions to come back with a good action picture. By the sixth inning, he still hadn't gotten his shot. His deadline was getting near.

As Cobb stood on first base following a single, Sears told Cobb of his problem. (Photographers were permitted to work on the field in those days.) "If I'm not back soon with a good picture, it's going to be my job," pleaded the photographer.

"Okay," said Cobb, "go over to third base right now. I'll give you your action shot."

As Sears hustled to the other side of the field, Cobb flashed the hit-and-run sign to George Moriarty at the plate. Cobb took off with the pitch and Moriarty singled behind him into right field. Cobb steamed around second and toward third. With his spikes flashing, he slid hard into third baseman Larry Gardner of the Red Sox. The umpire bellowed: "Safe!"

Sears got his picture. He nodded to Cobb, who was still on the ground, and headed for the exit gate.

Right from the start, Cobb was a different kind of player—certainly a different kind of personality.

He showed up in Detroit on the night of August 29, 1905, fresh out of the minor leagues. Nobody knew much about him. In fact, few people had ever heard of him. The newspapers called him "Cyrus Cobb."

When he arrived, he stood only five eleven and weighed just 160 pounds—not an imposing figure. He had a fair complexion with reddish-blond hair which was parted in the middle in the style of the day. With only one suitcase—containing his lone suit, underwear, and dirty laundry, his pancake-style glove, and several of his favorite bats—he looked like a country bumpkin, which is exactly what he was. He checked into a third-class hotel for ten dollars a week on the American plan—room and meals. The next day, Cobb walked to Bennett Park and signed a contract for $1,800 a year. He would receive only a fraction of that money because there was only one month left in the season.

Manager Bill Armour sat the recruit down in his office and asked him all sorts of questions. How old was he? Did he drink? Smoke? Chase girls? What did he hit at Augusta? Cobb told him, "I will be nineteen on December 18, I don't booze, smoke,

Nineteen-year-old Ty Cobb (right) listens to his first manager, straw-hatted Bill Armour. ◆

As a nineteen-year-old rookie, Ty Cobb prepares to smack the first of his 4,191 hits, the major league record until Pete Rose surpassed the number in 1985. ◆

or wench around. I batted .326 in 104 games in the South Atlantic League, with 60 runs scored and 40 stolen bases, and I bat left-handed and throw right-handed and I would appreciate it if I could get dressed now and go out on the field."

What young Ty did not tell Armour was that only three weeks earlier his father died under mysterious circumstances.

Armour liked the looks of his new rookie. "Okay, you play center field today. Be sure to check the sun and the wind."

Armour started to tell Cobb his signs.

Cobb stirred. "Can't I just play my own way?" the youngster said.

Armour looked at him and smiled. "Suit yourself, but no foul-ups out there," he said.

The New York Highlanders were in town and Jack Chesbro, the celebrated spitballer, was on the mound. "Don't try to kill his spitter," instructed Armour. "Just meet the ball."

Cobb nodded.

Armour inserted Cobb into the fifth spot in his batting order, an exalted position for a rookie.

When Cobb went to the plate for the first time, the fans quickly looked at their scorecards for his name. It wasn't listed. Cobb took his stance in the batter's box and glared out at Chesbro. He muttered something, just loud enough for the New York pitcher to hear.

Chesbro glowered back at him.

The New York pitching ace got two quick strikes on the rookie. Cobb swung at the next pitch and hit a line drive over the head of center fielder Eddie Hahn. It went for a double and drove in a runner from second base. The fans went wild. Cobb's long love-hate relationship with the Detroit faithful had begun.

Cobb infuriated his own teammates as much as he did the opposition. He acted as if there was only one way to play the game—his way—and wondered why the others couldn't do all the things he could do.

At first, only words were exchanged. The players would lock Cobb out of the hotel bathroom, leaving him to shiver in the corridor. They would push him aside at the batting cage. When he got back to the clubhouse, he would find his caps crushed out of shape and his bats sawed in half. The fisticuffs soon followed.

Cobb was better with his mouth and his feet than he was with his fists. He didn't win all his fights. He probably was under .500 in his unofficial ring career. Yet, he backed away from no man.

On a hot spring day in 1917, in Waxahachie, Texas, Cobb tangled with second baseman Buck Herzog of the New York

Giants during an exhibition game. They grappled at second base, rolling around on the ground like children in a schoolyard fight. Soon both teams were involved. Even Jim Thorpe, the big Indian who was playing center field for the Giants, got in on the scrap. That didn't keep Cobb from landing one solid shot on Herzog's jaw. After the game, Cobb thought no more about the altercation. He considered it over. Another day at the ballpark.

That night, during dinner at the hotel, Herzog approached Cobb's table and asked for a meeting when Cobb finished eating. "I want to see you in your room . . . and no swords and pistols."

Cobb looked up at him.

"If that's what you want, that's what you'll get," Cobb said. "I'll see you in thirty minutes."

Cobb proceeded to finish his meal, then went to his room, rolled up the rug, and moved the furniture to one side. Word of the impending fight spread throughout the hotel and the players gathered outside of Cobb's room.

Charles "Buck" Herzog was a New York Giants infielder when he tangled on the field with Ty Cobb and then lost a rematch in Cobb's hotel room later that night. ◆

Cobb peeked through his keyhole and saw that Herzog was wearing a khaki shirt, old pants, and a belt tightly drawn around his waist. He had rubber-soled shoes on his feet.

Cobb thought to himself: "Uh-oh . . . I might slip in my street shoes, but he'll have a firm grip with those rubber-soled shoes." Cobb calmly filled his water pitcher and wet down the floor. He knew his leather-soled shoes would grip the wet floor while Herzog's rubber-bottomed shoes would slip.

Cobb opened the door. "How would you like to fight?" he asked Herzog.

"Any way suits me," Herzog growled. "I may get licked, but I'm here to fight you."

Cobb smiled at Herzog. "You damn well know you're going to get licked," he said.

One story said that Herzog floored Cobb with his first punch. Cobb denied it in later years. He said, "Nothing of the sort happened. I missed my first punch, a right hook, but I hit him a full-swinging backhander and down he went."

Cobb went on, "I assure you this was no science on my part. I just got him a good one. He was on the floor and I reached down and grabbed him by the shirt and pulled him erect. I clipped him again . . . I'm not proud of this . . . but he went over backwards. From a kneeling position, he said, 'I've got enough . . . I've got enough.' "

Some of this powerful prose is surely exaggerated. But it is a fact that Cobb fought all through his life, trying to foist his will on those around him. Where he acquired such a belligerent attitude, nobody knows. Maybe it was inherent; or maybe it started with the death of his father.

Three weeks before Cobb was called up to the Tigers in 1905—August 8, to be exact—Cobb's family finished dinner at their Royston, Georgia, home. Cobb's father, County School Commissioner W. H. Cobb—Professor Cobb to his friends—hitched up his buggy in the barnyard. He said he had some business in a neighboring town and didn't know when he'd return.

Ty's mother went to bed but slept fitfully. She said she was awakened by some rustling noises outside her bedroom window. She reached for a pistol in a dresser drawer. She saw the silhouette of someone trying to open the window.

Gripped with fear, Amanda Cobb forced herself to the side of the window and pulled back the curtain to look outside. She saw a man standing there. She screamed and opened fire. The bullets struck the intruder in the head and stomach, and he toppled back onto the front porch. It was Professor Cobb, who slowly bled to death.

Cobb fathered five children and was remembered by his son James Howell Cobb as a strict disciplinarian who urged them on academically as well as athletically. ◆

An investigation followed, but no conclusions were reached since everyone seemed to have a different version of the shooting. According to town gossip, Professor Cobb had suspected his wife of infidelity and came back early to catch her in the act. Nothing was ever proven, except that young Ty Cobb became embittered about his mother's actions and never forgave her. From that moment on, it was as if he were driven by demons. He adopted a very hard and cynical outlook on life that never changed, not even on the day he died.

At the time of his father's death, Cobb was making quite a name for himself on the Augusta team of the Sally League. The Detroit Tigers trained in Augusta and the Tigers players saw how serious Cobb was. They poked fun at him. They told owner Frank Navin to come out and take a look at this gawky kid. It would be good for a laugh.

Navin didn't laugh.

He saw a young, raw-boned outfielder who could run like the wind. He saw how quickly Cobb got down the line to first base. He saw a young man of great potential.

The kid was crude, but look at him run.

Navin had a deal with the Augusta team whereby he would allow them the use of one of his players in return for the use of their ballpark during spring training. William J. Croke, owner of the Augusta team, picked pitcher Al Cicotte for the 1905 sea-

50

Cobb mastered every art with the bat, hit to all fields, smacked the long ball when challenged, and bunted expertly. ◆

son. Navin didn't think he was giving up much, since Cicotte weighed only 135 pounds. (Cicotte turned out to be a highly effective pitcher whose chance at the Hall of Fame vanished after he surfaced as a leading participant in the 1919 Black Sox scandal in which eight Chicago White Sox players conspired to dump the World Series.)

As part of the deal, Navin could have his pick of any player on the Augusta club at the end of the season for $500.

Ed Barrow, who was managing the Indianapolis team, had had a chance to buy Cobb and second baseman Clyde Engle earlier in the year. The Augusta club was asking $500 apiece, or $800 for the pair. Barrow wanted Cobb, but offered only $300. He was turned down. When the season was over, Navin asked for Cobb, and even threw in an extra $200 to seal the deal. Later, Barrow would lament: "I lost Ty Cobb for $200."

Cobb had played hard at Augusta, but wasn't a favorite with

SCRAPBOOK

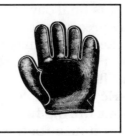

"Ty fought everybody on the Detroits until the other Tigers realized that all he wants to do is win baseball games. Then they get in back of him as solid as wet sand and Detroit cops the berries in 1907, '08, '09—and almost repeats in '10 and '11. But they go very bad in the spring of '12 and Cobb is sorer than ingrown hairs on a porcupine."

Arthur "Bugs" Baer, *The Crambury Tiger*

◆

"It is very embarrassing to be singled out as the one bright star on the Detroit baseball team. I want to tell you gentlemen that the Detroit baseball team is composed of stars, and these gentlemen sitting around the table are just as much entitled to words of praise as I am. One man does not make up the team. I am not the Detroit baseball team. I would like to see such stars as George Mullin, and George Moriarty, our captain, receive their share of praise."

Remarks by Ty Cobb at banquet in 1911

◆

"Ty Cobb has a big heart. The raw recruits on the spring trip found a good friend in the mighty Tyrus. Unlike many star ball players, Cobb does not try to lord it over the young fellows . . . rather Cobb likes to mingle with the youngsters."

C. D. Freiburger, *Detroit Journal*, 1911

◆

"In Boston, a huge weekday crowd . . . reviled Cobb all afternoon, hissing him, badgering him, throwing hard wads of paper at him. In the eighth inning, with Boston losing 5–1, Mays, pitching in relief, threw two fastballs close to Cobb's head. The two players went for each other, but the umpires and several policemen, thoughtfully provided for the occasion by the city, prevented a fight. When the shouts and threats subsided, Mays pitched again and hit Ty on the wrist, and the vituperation began all over again. When the game ended, some improper Bostonians came out of the stands and tried to get at Cobb, and the police had to escort him from the field."

Robert W. Creamer, *Babe: The Legend Comes to Life*

◆

"Cobb though—he was a very complex person—never did have many friends. Trouble was he had such a rotten disposition that it was damn hard to be his friend. . . . He antagonized so many people that hardly anyone would speak to him, even among his own teammates.

"Ty didn't have a sense of humor, see. Especially, he could never laugh at himself. Consequently, he took a lot of things the wrong way. What would usually be an innocent-enough wisecrack would become cause for a fist fight if Ty was involved . . ."

Davy Jones to Lawrence S. Ritter, *The Glory of Their Times*

◆

the fans. On his final day, the town's officials wanted to give him a going-away present. Not many sons of Georgia went up to the big leagues. Led by the mayor, they marched to home plate and gave Ty a gold watch for good luck.

Cobb was flustered. He wasn't accustomed to kindness or generosity. He fumbled for words, and finally said he would thank everyone during his final game in Augusta, but he struck out in his last time at bat.

A fan cried out: "Let Detroit have him."

It is easy to understand why so many people despised Cobb. He knew he was good, and he let everyone else know it. He was forever showing up people, both on and off the field. Violence seemed to follow him everywhere. In Philadelphia, a fan ran on the field and pressed a gun to Cobb's stomach. Cobb stared him down, daring him to pull the trigger. He was mugged by three hoods in Detroit, but knocked two of them out with his fists. In Cleveland, he was charged with stabbing a hotel porter.

Nobody questioned his toughness. Once, in Toledo, his tonsils flared up and he went to a doctor to have them removed. The doctor operated without the aid of any anesthetics. Cobb would open his mouth and the doctor would chop away. Cobb would

Ty Cobb beating Lou Criger, the famous old Boston catcher, in a play at the plate. Criger is tagging Cobb but Cobb's foot has already touched the plate and Billy Evans, the umpire who is running up, is calling him safe. In the foreground is Hughie Jennings, manager of the Tigers during their pennant-winning years. ◆

spit out the blood and the doctor would chop away again. "He cut me seven times," Cobb would say later on. "I lost so much blood I nearly fainted." The next day he played seven innings.

Cobb was a clever businessman. He invested in Coca-Cola and General Motors before those companies became worldwide giants, and he became a millionaire many times over.

When the end drew near for the great man, he entered Emory Hospital in Atlanta. He brought more than $1 million in negotiable bonds with him, placed them on the nightstand, and weighted them down with a pistol.

Ty Cobb died on July 17, 1961. He was 74. He was entombed in the family vault in Royston, Georgia. Only two players showed up at his funeral—Ray Schalk and Mickey Cochrane.

Ed Barrow served as field marshal for the Detroit Base Ball Club in 1903 and for the first months of the following season. His one star was outfielder Sam Crawford. Barrow, who discovered Honus Wagner a decade earlier, later transformed Babe Ruth from a pitcher to an outfielder and brought him to the New York Yankees where Barrow's front office maneuvers helped build the Yankees into a dynasty. But he missed out on Ty Cobb. ◆

Harry Sanders, age 92, an automobile dealer and boyhood friend of Ty Cobb, sits on the steps of Ty's mausoleum in Royston, Georgia. Cobb's father, an educator whom the locals called "Professor," named his son in honor of the stalwart resistance of the city of Tyre when besieged by the armies of Alexander the Great in the fourth century B.C. ◆

THE BOOKKEEPER

◆

Bob Fothergill was a dumpy, friendly man who could murder the ball. He was an outfielder with the Tigers all through the 1920s, and he loved his life as a ballplayer, especially the eating part. He grew to such proportions that the fans in the bleachers would razz him by shouting, "When does the balloon go up?"

Poor Fats. He was only five ten but he weighed between 230 and 240 pounds and always took a lot of kidding about his size. After he hit .367 in 1926, he felt it was time to go in and talk to owner Frank Navin about a big raise.

The Bookkeeper saw him coming.

That's what they called Navin—the man who watched over his books as carefully as he watched over his players. He was the first of the influential owners of the Tigers, and he was pretty much a one-man operation.

He was the owner, general manager, business manager, farm director, and publicity director. If it got busy downstairs, he'd go into one of the ticket booths and sell admissions. He kept an accounting of the day's receipts in his vest pocket. He ran the club with an iron fist from 1907 until his death in 1935.

He was ready for Fothergill.

It was an unseasonably hot day, but Navin closed all the windows and turned up the steam radiators. He was usually abrupt with his players but when Fothergill entered his office, he said, "Come in, come in, Bob. Sit down. Have a seat. It's good to see you."

Fothergill knew something was up, but he didn't know what.

Navin started rambling. He talked about everything imaginable—the weather, the new cars coming off the assembly lines,

A bookkeeper's gimlet eye hid Navin's genius for discerning talent and the affection he had for many of his employees. ◆

Bob "Fats" Fothergill was celebrated for his eating and derided for his glovework in the outfield during the 1920s. But he was a lifetime .326 batter. ♦

the state of the nation . . . everything except Fothergill's .367 batting average. The room started heating up and so did Fat Bob. The sweat began pouring off him. Navin talked on and on.

Finally, Navin pulled a contract from his desk drawer, put it in front of Fothergill, and kept jabbering away. Fat Bob grabbed a pen, signed it, and rushed out—desperate to get out of that sweatbox. The contract was for several thousand dollars less than he had intended to ask for.

Navin was not quite the pinchpenny many thought him to be, but neither was he in the habit of giving his money away. He operated the Tigers through some very lean years but managed to stay in business. He usually showed a small profit—not an easy thing to do, particularly in the 1930s.

He was also known as "Mr. Poker Face."

He rarely smiled, seldom laughed, and couldn't have cried if he were paid to do it. He showed little emotion at a ball game. It didn't matter if the Tigers were winning or losing, he always wore the same blank expression on his face. He knew the game better than most, but did not involve himself in the emotional end of it. Some say he adopted this straight-faced manner as a young croupier in a gambling house. That's where he learned to look on the games with apparent disinterest; as he raked in the chips for the house, he knew smiling was not allowed.

Frank Navin was one of the great characters in the history of baseball in Detroit.

Few know that today—or even care. But the simple truth is that he was the man who built the foundation for the Detroit franchise. He helped the Tigers get established in the early 1900s. He brought Ty Cobb to Detroit. He sighed Hughie Jennings, the first great manager of the Tigers. He went to Connie Mack in Philadelphia, bought Mickey Cochrane, put him in charge of the team, and brought Detroit its first world championship in 1935. Frank Navin may have been one of the most misunderstood men of all time.

Even though he was portrayed as a cold and dispassionate man, he was a warm and friendly person, exceedingly loyal, a man who loved life and had a whimsical sense of humor. He was one of the most charitable owners of his time—a time when baseball owners were not noted for their philanthropic tendencies.

One day while Navin sat in his office talking to a friend, there was a knock on the door. "Who is it?" he asked.

"Santa Claus."

"Who?"

"Santa Claus."

Navin rose. He opened the door and who should be standing there but The Man himself—beard, red suit, jingling a bell and holding a small box in his hand.

Navin wondered how this man had gotten past the front desk, but he decided to go along with the gag. "Hello, Santa Claus," he said. "How are you? I haven't seen you in a long time."

"Ho, ho, ho," said Santa Claus, holding the box out to Navin. It was a collection box.

Navin reached into his pocket, pulled out some bills and stuffed them into the slot on top of the box.

"Thank you," said Santa Claus. "I hope you have a merry Christmas."

As Santa backed out the door, Navin broke into a soft smile. His companion said, "I think you were just had."

Navin went over to the window and pulled back the drapes. He looked into the street and saw the Santa Claus talking to another Santa Claus. He saw them open the box and divide the money between themselves. He opened the window and yelled down to them, "I hope you two are having a good Christmas season."

They looked up and waved to him. "We'll take care of Christmas, you take care of the Tigers." Then they walked away.

Navin closed the drapes, turned to his companion, and said, "Santa Clauses have to eat, too."

Navin—in his own way—was as colorful as any of his players. But not many knew it.

He never smoked in his life, and never drank. He didn't chew or swear. He didn't object to others doing these things, he just

(Left) Navin brought a certain sartorial style to the rough-hewn seats of Navin Field during the 1930s.

(Right) Navin escorted some female friends to the 1933 Kentucky Derby. His pal Judge Landis, who attempted to boot Rogers Hornsby out of baseball for betting on horses, ignored Navin's addiction to wagering. ◆

didn't want to be a part of them himself. His great loves were horses and the racetrack.

Navin told everyone he wasn't superstitious, but if he ever saw a cross-eyed person at the track, he wouldn't make any bets that day. He always put his left shoe on first. He had his own notions about nutrition. He wouldn't eat pork because he felt it wasn't good for him. He never ate spinach, but was forever sneaking ice cream and candy.

He knew all of the industrialists in Detroit and belonged to eight clubs at one time—the Detroit Athletic Club, Detroit Riding and Hunt Club, Bloomfield Open Hunt Club, Bloomfield Country Club, Detroit Golf Club, Ponchartrain Club, Detroit Yacht Club, and the Recess Club. He did not own a boat or golfing equipment, and never swam. His favorite pastime was playing bridge. He liked good movies as well as stage plays, and he went horseback riding every day of his life. He owned six racehorses, much to the annoyance of Commissioner Kenesaw Mountain Landis, a man who felt baseball and horse racing did not mix. Yet Landis and Navin were close friends, and Landis always sought Navin's advice in matters of baseball.

Navin wore tortoiseshell glasses and his desk was always in order. He kept two pictures of his wife, Grace, in front of him

Along with his friend and ally, Commissioner Kenesaw Mountain Landis, Navin brought his derby and Kewpie doll look to the 1933 World Series to watch the New York Giants beat the Washington Senators. ◆

at all times. Navin was the quietest—and perhaps the most respected—of all the owners in baseball. Not once did the Tigers finish last under his leadership.

"He would sit silent for hours at meetings while arguments raged all around him," said H. G. Salsinger, the longtime sports editor of the *Detroit News.* "They would finally ask for his opinion and he always came up with the solution to their problems."

Salsinger was a confidant of Navin's. In fact, he was the man who suggested that Navin buy Mickey Cochrane and make him manager of the Tigers in 1934. It was a move that would result in two pennants and a world championship for Detroit.

Salsinger wrote: "Navin was one of the few owners who knew the playing end of the game as well as he knew the business end. Few of his players ever matched him in his understanding of the technical aspects of the game. He made a study of baseball and knew more about pitching than anyone around. He never criticized his players, except if he felt they were lazy and weren't putting out their best effort. For this reason, they liked playing for him. None of them got rich but they always felt he was fair in dealing with them.

"He did not make friends easily, but once you got to know him, you could see his rare sense of humor. And he was one of the most charitable men around, always helping those who needed help, especially former players who were down on their luck."

Yet, despite his generosity with others, the money battles between Navin and Cobb have become legend. They fought almost constantly. They haggled over dollars and cents when Cobb was a player and later when he was a manager.

But Cobb knew how to squeeze Navin, as well.

Cobb was negotiating his contract with Navin at the Vanderbilt Hotel in New York. They met in a downstairs room. Upstairs, in another room, sat George Weiss. Weiss was the boss of the Yankees and badly wanted Cobb to play for him.

Every time Navin made an offer, Cobb would go right to the phone and call Weiss's room. He would tell Weiss the figure and ask him if he could match it.

Weiss kept raising it.

Each time Cobb relayed the Yankee offer to Navin, Navin increased his offer.

This went on for about an hour—and the ploy worked. Cobb got his $50,000 for the 1926 season, his last with the Tigers. But he hadn't heard the last of Navin on the subject.

Cobb had been with the Tigers since 1905, and the city of Detroit wanted to honor him at a banquet. Two rooms were set

Navin engineered a trade with Washington for Senators' manager Stanley "Bucky" Harris, who could not raise the Tigers above fifth place in five seasons. ◆

aside at the Statler Hotel in downtown Detroit. Gifts arrived from everywhere. The city itself intended to present Cobb with a $1,000 hall clock. The Tigers, of course, were also expected to reward Cobb with a gift—naturally, the finest of all.

Navin called Cobb aside before the banquet. He told him he was in a bind: Cobb had just signed a $50,000 contract with the Tigers, but Navin explained that this was the same amount that American League president Ban Johnson earned. Navin said it would look bad for a player to be earning as much as the league president, so if Cobb would sign a $40,000 contract, Navin would give him the other $10,000 as a bonus.

"Do what you want," sneered Cobb, and walked away.

That night, at the climax of the banquet, Navin stood up before 2,000 people and delivered a heartrending speech about Ty Cobb and what he meant to his team and to the city of Detroit. With a grand flourish, he announced that he had a $10,000 check as a token of his appreciation for the great man and great ballplayer.

Navin, despite his milquetoast manner, was not afraid to stand up to Cobb.

Navin and Cobb had a memorable (nonfinancial) run-in during the 1918 season.

Ty Cobb in 1917 hit .383 and Frank Navin paid him $20,000 for his services. Sportswriter H. G. Salsinger estimated that the shrewd outfielder earned another $30,000 from activities off the field. At the conclusion of the war-shortened 1918 season, Cobb took a commission in the Chemical Warfare Service. Although the Great War would end within a few weeks, Cobb went to France where he participated in a gas warfare drill. The men were accidentally exposed to poison gas and Captain Christy Mathewson, the superb New York Giants pitcher in the unit, suffered severe lung damage. Cobb escaped with minor discomfort. ◆

Cobb was in a slump, and instead of just being difficult, he became impossible. The Boston Red Sox were in town and Ray Collins was pitching. Cobb did not hit well against Collins, so he decided to sit the game out. But he needed an unimpeachable excuse. Cobb seized on an argument with teammate Davy Jones over a hit-and-run play. The sulking Cobb blamed Jones for missing a sign, and said he wouldn't be seen on the same field with him anymore. That was Cobb's way of avoiding Ray Collins.

Navin summoned Cobb to his office.

"I'm not playing with Jones," Cobb fumed. "That bonehead can't even see the hit-and-run sign."

Navin scolded: "Oh, come on, Ty, suppose he did miss the sign. The other players tell me he didn't, but so what if he did? That's no reason for you not to play. You're just making an excuse because you're not hitting."

"Who told you that?" demanded Cobb.

"Never mind who told me," said Navin. "It's none of your business. You're going to play today and I don't want to hear any more about it. If you still refuse, I'm going to suspend you without pay. What's more, we're not taking Jones out of the lineup. That's out of the question."

Cobb left Navin's office. He was angry. He went to manager Hughie Jennings and told him he would play but he would play second base instead of the outfield. Why second base, nobody knew. It was just Cobb's way of forcing his will on others.

Jennings went along with his star. Jennings always went along with him. He listed Cobb as his second baseman, and Cobb looked like a bush-leaguer at the strange position.

When the game was over, Eddie Collins, the great Red Sox second baseman, sat down in the Boston clubhouse, wrote a letter to Navin, and put a dollar in the envelope. Collins wrote: "I am ashamed to have all that fun out of watching the great Ty Cobb try to play second base without paying for it."

Frank Navin makes sure C. B. White, of the White Star Refining Co., signs on the right line for the 1935 broadcast contract. ◆

Navin chortled at the letter and put the dollar in his desk.

Harry Heilmann, another of the great Detroit sluggers, claimed that only one person had ever gotten the best of Frank Navin. That was Mrs. Patrick McCafferty, an elderly woman who lived in one of the frame houses across the street from the ball-park.

She showed up in Navin's office one day holding the shattered pieces of a lamp. "Your ballplayers did this!" she exclaimed.

She said one of the players had hit a ball through the front window of her house, and the ball had smashed the lamp. She said the lamp had cost her $75 and was practically brand new.

Suspicious by nature, Navin carefully examined the broken lamp. He was looking for the sticker price on it. He found it at the base and then called for his accountant to make out a check for $75, payable to Mrs. Patrick McCafferty.

"Thank you, sir," the lady said. "You are a very fair man."

When she left, Navin blew up. "A broken lamp for $75—I've been robbed," he said.

The next day, Heilmann was walking around in downtown Detroit and passed a furniture store. He looked in the window and saw an exact duplicate of Mrs. McCafferty's lamp. His curiosity got the best of him and he went inside and asked the clerk if he might see the lamp in the window. He turned it over and looked at the sticker price. It was $7.50. Mrs. McCafferty had added a zero and moved the decimal point over one place.

The 1929 Tigers, with five .300 hitters, led the league in batting and finished sixth. With shrewd moves, Navin would have them back on top in five years. ◆

S C R A P B O O K

"I remember Mr. Navin telling me one time I was having a good year hitting and the last two weeks I slumped off badly and when the next spring come he said, 'Geeze, we'd 've played another two weeks I wouldn't have had to pay you as much.' "

Charlie Gehringer to Rod Roberts, 1985

♦

"Tall and corpulent, almost totally bald although he was only in his mid-thirties, Navin was a colorless, taciturn man who viewed the world impassively behind his horn-rimmed spectacles. His appearance and manner prompted some of the Tiger ballplayers to call him 'the Chinaman'— behind his back."

Charles C. Alexander, *Ty Cobb*

♦

"Navin pinched as many pennies as he could, with the result that he had one of the lowest payrolls in the big leagues. To be sure, nobody anywhere was drawing down a huge amount of money. In 1906, Bobby Wallace, the veteran shortstop of the St. Louis Browns, was the highest-salaried player in the majors at $6,500 annually. Navin, though, seems to have been exceptionally zealous in holding down costs. He was convinced, for example, that Sam Crawford, his top player, was worth no more than $2,700 for 1905, and he urged Crawford to accept his 'very liberal offer' and 'treat the club right.' . . . To Bobby Lowe, a utility infielder-outfielder nearing the end of a long and frequently illustrious career, Navin maintained that $1,800 for 1905 was 'the very best we will do.' That sum, incidentally, was also as much as Navin paid himself for four years."

Charles C. Alexander, *Ty Cobb*

♦

On the other hand, Navin could lose large sums of money at the racetrack and think nothing of it.

Once he got a tip and put $5,000 on an 8 to 1 shot at the track across the river in Windsor, Ontario. It was the first race on the program and he stood to win $40,000. When the barrier went up, it knocked the jockey out of the saddle, and Navin's horse was left at the starting line.

Navin simply looked down at his program and said, "I wonder what's good in the second race?"

Shortly after signing Cobb, Navin's teams won the American League pennant in 1907, 1908, and 1909, but were defeated in each of the World Series. He always told his friends, "I'd like to win one World Series before I die."

After the Tigers were beaten by the St. Louis Cardinals in the 1934 World Series, they got back into the Series again against the Chicago Cubs in 1935. And this time the Tigers finally made it all the way under Navin. They won their first World Series, four games to two, and the town went wild, celebrating long into the night.

Navin felt vindicated. More important, he felt happy. His life was complete. Five weeks later, he suffered a heart attack while riding one of his horses, and fell to the ground dead.

Fittingly, tigers guard the mausoleum containing Frank Navin's remains at the Holy Sepulchre Cemetery. ◆

Beginning in 1916, Harry Heilmann teamed with Cobb to restore the Tigers' one-two punch that had faded with Sam Crawford's decline. When not in the outfield, Heilmann played a graceful first base. ◆

DEPRESSION DAYS

◆

Nineteen thirty-four was a terrible year in Detroit. The Depression had hit the city as hard as any in the country—certainly harder than most. The assembly lines slowed down and all but came to a halt. Men were laid off everywhere. Workers stood by the front gates of the factories, huddled around fires, wondering when they would be allowed back in; wondering how they could support their families; wondering how they could even buy dinner for their families. Some did, indeed, take to selling apples on street corners.

Curiously enough, there was one place in town that seemed to be insulated from the grim realities of the day: the ballpark. Navin Field. Exciting things were happening at the corner of Michigan and Trumbull. The Tigers, a fifth-place team that drew only 320,972 fans in 1933, were winning ball games and challenging for the pennant.

Suddenly, people forgot that the rent was due or that they couldn't make this month's car payment. They took the trolley to Michigan and Trumbull and began filling the ballpark day after day. The attendance soared to 919,191 in 1934 and went over the one-million mark in 1935.

Although one of the smaller major league towns, and heavily struck by the Great Depression, Detroit during these years accounted for more than one-quarter of baseball's total number of paying customers.

"It was a little different than it is today," said Charlie Gehringer, the second baseman of that era. "Everybody dressed like they were going to the theater or maybe to church. Nobody wore jackets or jeans. We played in the afternoons (usually at three o'clock), and the lawyers would come out from their offices and they would be all spiffed up. The women in the box seats looked

Lynwood "Schoolboy" Rowe towered 6'4½" on the mound, winning 24 games in '34 and 19 in both of the following seasons. Just before the 1934 World Series, the diffident Rowe appeared on a radio interview and ad libbed to his wife at home, "How'm I doin', Edna?" Whenever Rowe pitched, the Cardinal bench greeted him with raucous cries of "How'm I doin', Edna?" ◆

Unemployed men hungrily consume the fare at a soup kitchen. Detroit was especially hard hit during the Depression; thousands were laid off as the demand for the city's industrial products was dramatically curtailed. ◆

just beautiful. You'd think they were there for a garden party."

And, of course, there were the bleacherites, seated in left field and making a racket from start to finish at every game. They were a rowdy lot and were there to let off some steam.

Baseball was pretty much the only game in town in that summer of 1934. A pro football team, destined to become the Detroit Lions, was coming in from a place called Portsmouth, Ohio, but it wasn't there yet. There was a hockey team that in its few brief years of operation had been known first as the Cougars, then as the Falcons, and finally as the Red Wings. The people from across the river in Windsor, Ontario, seemed to be more interested in the hockey team than those who lived in Detroit. Baseball is what everyone talked about, and it was a good feeling: with the team winning for a change, there was a reason to feel some pride in the city.

The team was truly a collection of characters. Mickey Cochrane, the bold, bandy-legged playing manager—"Black Mike," they called him—would be shouting orders from behind home plate. They listened to him, too; nobody ever crossed Black Mike. He tolerated no nonsense out there. The Goose—Leon Goslin— would be out in left field, slowly tapping his glove while waiting for the next play. He always tapped his glove between pitches.

Billy Rogell, the hawk-nosed shortstop, would peer intently at the pitcher and catcher, waiting for the play to begin. He reminded you so much of Honus Wagner, the legendary Dutchman from Pittsburgh. The big guy, Hank Greenberg—a gangling man, awkward in his manner—was bent over at first base, awaiting the next ground ball. Ground balls were always an adventure for the hulking first baseman. And over at second, the lean, intense-looking man with his cap fixed tightly on his head stood there motionless, like a statue in the park. Nothing ever bothered Charlie Gehringer, labeled "the mechanical man" because of his unfailing consistency.

There should have been resentment toward these men, who were making a good living by playing a boy's game at such a difficult time. Just the opposite was true. The fans, needing an outlet from all the worries of the day, embraced them as heroes. At least they could go to the ballpark and know there was still some normality in the world. An afternoon at Navin Field, with

The corner of Michigan and Trumbull is the address of the grand old ballpark, Navin Field. An aerial view shows a capacity crowd for a 1934 World Series game. ◆

Gehringer shooting a double into the right-field corner and with Greenberg, up next, putting one into the left center-field bleachers, was a reason to feel good. It was a reason to feel hopeful, too: if the ball club could survive, why couldn't the people of the city? The banks could close, but not the ballpark. Besides, it cost only a buck to get in, fifty cents for a seat in the bleachers.

The players were untouched by the Depression, and that was fine with everyone. They represented a symbol of hope for those down on their luck.

"I knew things were tough on the outside," said Greenberg, "but I was young and trying to make my own way in life. We all knew what was going on, but we couldn't do anything about it. We just did our own jobs the best way we knew how. We knew that everyone was behind us and that was a good feeling. To be honest about it, I'd have to say the Depression didn't touch us at all."

Life was simply different in those days. Greenberg remembered a nickel being a big tip. That's what the players tipped at

The bleacherites cheer for the Tigers at an early World Series game. A loud and loyal crew, many bleacherites found escape in the Tigers from the harsh realities of the Depression. ◆

"Impetuous fighting blood, pugnacious application and charging, fiery, indomitable spirit that knows no signal for retreat, led the spike-shod feet of Mickey Cochrane up from the farmlands of New England to major league fame and glory."

—Bill Dooly, Philadelphia *Record* ♦

Hall of Famer "Goose" Goslin broke in with the Washington Senators in 1921 and compiled a lifetime batting average of .316 with a high watermark of .379 to lead the league in 1928. Although his single won the 1935 Series for the Tigers, his best championship achievements were for the Senators in '24 and '25 when he cracked three round-trippers on both occasions. ♦

"After watching me hit and field out at second base, he (Ty Cobb) climbed up to Mr. Navin's office—this was with his uniform and spikes on—and got Mr. Navin down to watch me. . . . they signed me up.

—Charlie Gehringer, *Baseball for the Love of It* ◆

Anything but a natural at fielding, Hank Greenberg laboriously learned his position, only to be shifted to the outfield to make a place for slugger Rudy York. When he heard of the change, Greenberg, at his own expense, traveled to six spring training camps to consult veteran outfielders on how they handled the position. But it was with his bat that he spoke most clearly: 331 homers, including 58 in 1938 and a lifetime average of .313. He lost almost four productive years to World War II and on his return from service in 1945, his late season heroics drove the Tigers to a pennant and World Series title. ◆

dinner. It was the accepted practice.

"The big deal was whether you wanted to eat dinner at the Leland Hotel in downtown Detroit," he said. "They served a complete dinner and an orchestra played while you ate, and you had to decide if all of this was worth a dollar twenty-five. I thought about it a lot and finally said to myself, 'Aw, what the hell—let's give it a try.' You also had to leave a quarter tip, so that made it a pretty expensive evening. I decided to try it, but I've got to admit I did it because they had an attractive waitress there, and I thought I could impress her with a twenty-five-cent tip."

Most of the players in those days were bachelors. Few could afford to be married, and fewer still had gone to college. They were single guys who came out of high school and began playing baseball in the minor leagues.

"So what we did," said Greenberg, "was look for cheap hotels to stay at. When I first came to Detroit, I stayed at the Wolverine Hotel, for eight bucks a week. They gave you a room with a bed but no closets. It was no problem. We just hung our clothes on the curtain rod in the bathroom. In fact, we could even steam our clothes in there, and that saved us a little more money. Since we took most of our showers at the ballpark, our bathrooms in the hotel became our closets."

Greenberg was different from most of the players on the Tigers. In a sense he was different from everyone in the league. He

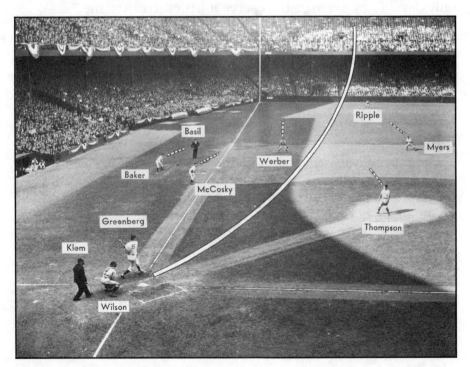

The typical path of a Greenberg blast, here a game-winning upper-deck shot against the Cincinnati Reds. ◆

Frank Navin started in the Detroit front office as club secretary in the first years of the franchise. William H. Yawkey, a multimillionaire, owned the team, but preferred the life of a playboy in New York City. After Navin assumed financial control of the Tigers, he built a new stadium in 1912, but player relations during his regime, which lasted into the 1930s, were marked by a tight grip on the wallet. ♦

was one of the very few Jewish ballplayers around. This presented no particular problem away from the field. He was embraced by the Jewish community in Detroit and made friends all over the city. He was always invited to dinner at the best Jewish homes and country clubs in the area. He was a true hero to the Jewish population, which was considerable in those days.

On the field, his religion was another matter. A boy from the Bronx, he would have been a natural asset to a New York club with that city's large Jewish poulation. But at first base the Giants had Bill Terry, the National League's last .400 hitter, and the Yankees had the indomitable Lou Gehrig. The Brooklyn Dodgers were content with Sam Leslie.

Greenberg was the target of slurs wherever the Tigers played. Ironically, the Yankees gave him the worst time of all. "They always had a couple of guys in the dugout who were on me all the time," said Greenberg. "It got pretty nasty. One time they even brought up a player from the minor leagues just to give me a hard time. I thought I handled it pretty well. I never let them know they were getting to me. That way, they would have won. But it wasn't easy. I could take it because I saw others getting it, too. Italians were 'wops,' Germans were 'krauts,' and Polish players were 'dumb Polacks.' Me, I was a 'kike,' a 'sheenie,' or a 'mockie.' I was a good target. What made it tough is that there were a lot of Italians, Germans, and Poles around, but I was the only Jew. They seemed to reserve a little extra for me."

Greenberg had an outstanding season in 1934. He batted .339, with 26 homers and 139 runs batted in. As his stature grew, so did his standing in the community. Whole families wanted to adopt him as their son, and they let it be known that their prettiest daughters were available for dates. At Joe Muer's seafood restaurant, they held a corner table for High Henry and kept it guarded by an extra waiter because they knew he liked to dine in peace.

Greenberg was an astute businessman from his earliest days as a player. In later years, he became a millionaire as an investment broker. But right from the beginning he understood the financial aspects of baseball.

He lived in New York City, and after his banner season in 1934, he got a call from Frank Navin, owner of the Tigers. Navin was at the Commodore Hotel in New York for the baseball meetings. He wanted Greenberg to come downtown and talk about his 1935 contract. Though Navin considered himself a frugal man, many branded him a cheapskate. He guarded his dollars with a miserly devotion: a dollar in your pocket meant a dollar out of his pocket.

Greenberg had hit .301 as a rookie in 1933, but Navin had told him he might be a fluke, and he didn't want to be stuck with flukes. He paid him $5,500 in 1934. Navin had told Greenberg, "You've got to prove you can hit major league pitching two years in a row."

The next year Greenberg was nervous when he went into Navin's hotel room. Navin wasted no time and said, "What do you want in 1935?"

"I'd like to have $15,000," said Greenberg.

Navin stirred in his chair. "Very well," he said. "I'll give you a $10,000 contract and $5,000 bonus."

"I don't care how you do it," said Greenberg, "but my contract will be for $15,000 and that's where we'll start talking next season."

Navin harrumphed. "Very well," he said. "We'll do it your way."

Greenberg was holding his breath, but didn't dare show any signs of nervousness. Navin took out his ledger and wrote Greenberg a check for $5,000.

Greenberg felt a chill go through his body. He had never seen that much money at one time before. It scared him.

When he walked out of the hotel, he saw a bank directly across the street.

"No way was I going to take any chance with that money," he said. "I lived away up in the Bronx and I had to take the subway home. I went into the bank and opened a savings account and deposited the whole $5,000."

When Charlie Gehringer joined the Tigers in 1924, life was simpler. Newspapers were two cents, the movies a nickel. You could buy a good used car for $350. Gehringer, who came to Detroit from the farmlands of Fowlerville, Michigan, was never comfortable in the big city. He lived with a family in a private home on Pingree and 12th Street, and took the trolley to the ballpark. He paid ten dollars a week for a room and three meals a day, and the family treated him like their own son. Gehringer liked this setup because the family had two sons and he could pal around with them at night, playing cards, going to the picture show, or sitting on the back porch, talking. He did not like hotel life, though he did live downtown during the Christmas season to work in the sporting goods department at J. L. Hudson's department store.

By the time Greenberg showed up in 1933, Gehringer was a fixture in the Detroit lineup. He was considered the best second baseman in the game.

"I was a bush-leaguer compared to him," said Greenberg. "I idolized him, and we got along fine. We never hung out together because Charlie was more comfortable with the older players.

"Gomez (Vernon, 'Lefty') gave me the nickname 'mechanical man.' He said, 'You wind him up in the spring and he goes all summer, hits .330 or .340 or whatever, and then you shut him off in the fall.' "

Charlie Gehringer— Unpublished interview with Rod Roberts ♦

What got me is that everything seemed so easy for him. In fact, I resented him a little, because everything was so easy for him and so hard for me. He'd catch everything in the field and get two or three hits. Me, it was a terror going to the ballpark. I wondered how I'd mess up next. A bad day for Charlie would be one strikeout—*one strikeout*! I'd be flailing away at the ball, looking very foolish at the plate, and I kept getting my feet tangled up at first base. I could never figure out when to go for ground balls between first and second. I wanted to catch everything so I could prove I could do the job, so I was going for balls I had no right to even try for. I'd dive for one and it would bounce off my glove and go into right field. Charlie would be standing there. He wouldn't be mad or anything. He'd just say, 'I could have gotten that one.' The man was amazing. After a while, I stayed at first base and let him field everything."

Gehringer has his own memories of those marvelous days in the 1930s. For instance, they didn't have any beer in the club-house. The beer came later, after the players dressed and left the ballpark.

"Our guys loved beer, but it was no big deal that we didn't have it in the clubhouse," said Gehringer. "We'd drink water or maybe orange juice. We might have had some Cokes, I don't remember. But in those days we didn't have any fancy soft drinks, like 7-Up or Orange Crush."

They had no drugs either. "Not even pain pills," said Gehringer. "If something hurt, you either played with it or ran some hot water on it in the shower. Nobody ever wanted to come out of the lineup. There were always three guys who wanted to take your place."

Gehringer played nineteen years with the Tigers and batted .320. Like Greenberg, he went into the Hall of Fame when his playing days were done.

Born on May 11, 1903, Gehringer will be 86 years old in 1989. He was stunned when High Henry Greenberg died in 1986 at the age of 75.

"I honestly thought I would go before him," Gehringer said in a quiet moment in his home in northwest Detroit, where he lives with his wife, Jo. "Hank always seemed so healthy. He was such a great competitor, I thought he would last longer than any of us."

These two—Greenberg and Gehringer—were known as the "G-Men" of Detroit. They were an awesome pair. Gehringer would get on base and Greenberg would knock him home. Greenberg would say to Gehringer, "Now, Charlie, just get them around to third—I'll send them in." And send them in, he did. He knocked

Shortstop Billy Rogell played seven full seasons in the mid-1930's, collaborating with second baseman Charlie Gehringer. At his position, he led the league in fielding 1935–1937. ♦

in 170 runs when the Tigers won the pennant and World Series in 1935, and he knocked in 183 runs in 1937. Greenberg finished his thirteen-year career with a .313 average, but he loved those RBIs as much as he loved life. He finished with 1,276 RBIs in 1,394 games, a remarkable average of nearly one a game.

Gehringer was a quiet man. He remained a bachelor all through his playing days. His mother was a diabetic and he felt it was his responsibility to take care of her. He did not think there was room for two women in his life, so he was loyal to his mother throughout her life.

"Oh, there were some nice girls around, but my mother had trouble getting around and I couldn't see bringing another woman into that situation," Gehringer said. "We lived together in the off-season, and my mother took good care of me. She was a great cook, and we'd always have those German meals with those terrific desserts. I had a brother who lived a few blocks away, and a sister in the suburbs of Detroit, so we were never alone. We always had somebody over at the house."

Gehringer said that the Depression did not touch his household. He was earning a regular salary and, being a conservative man to begin with, he always had some money put aside in case of emergencies.

"I remember one year that Mr. Navin had to borrow money from the bank to take us to spring training," Gehringer recalled. "But we always got paid on time. We were lucky to always have a job. I knew a lot of people were out of work and some were going hungry. It was a terrible time but I didn't know what to do about it."

Navin fretted about his finances all through the Depression. He was a bookkeeper by nature and red ink made his blood run cold. He had seen his attendance drop to an average of 4,197 per game in 1933, and knew he had to do something to stimulate the public, particularly in the troubled times that were gripping the city. He hit upon a bold idea: he would try to get Babe Ruth from the Yankees and make him his manager in 1934.

Ruth was still the greatest drawing card in the game, even though he was 39 and slowing down. He could offer a diversion to the fans in Detroit. Navin thought fans might even pay to see him take batting practice before the games.

Navin asked his friend Jake Ruppert, the beer baron owner of the Yankees, for permission to talk to Ruth. Ruppert was only too happy to oblige. Ruth was becoming a burden to him. As

Long-retired Cobb met with another baseball legend, Babe Ruth, whom Navin tried to hire to manage the Tigers in 1933. While they played against one another, Cobb rode the Yankee slugger viciously and the two nearly fought on the field. ◆

Ruth's skills began to wane, he became more and more demanding.

Navin contacted Ruth by telephone and asked him if he could come to Detroit to talk about the job of managing the Tigers. To his astonishment, Ruth told Navin he didn't have the time. He said he was on his way to Hawaii for a vacation.

"Can't it wait until I get back?" Ruth asked.

"No, it can't," said Navin, miffed at the rebuff.

Ruth took his tour of the Pacific but at the suggestion of his business manager, Christy Walsh, he made several contacts with Navin through the mail. Ruth told Navin he was interested in the job but said he would have to have a large salary and a percentage of the gate. Navin cooled on the idea. He wasn't giving up any of his ball club, even to a man as popular as Babe Ruth.

But he was still without a manager.

Meanwhile, strange things were happening in Philadelphia.

Connie Mack, owner of the A's, was feeling the effects of the Depression as much as anyone in baseball. His situation was more acute than most, because his team was filled with star players who were making big bucks after winning the championship in 1929, '30, and '31. He wanted to dump some of these players just as he had unloaded his $100,000 infield fifteen years earlier. Word went out that ace pitcher Lefty Grove and veteran catcher Mickey Cochrane could be had for $200,000. Navin didn't have that kind of money and asked Mr. Mack if he could buy one for $100,000.

Here, a newspaperman stepped in and changed the course of baseball history in Detroit. H. G. Salsinger, longtime sports editor of the *Detroit News*, was a confidant of Navin. When the Tiger owner told him about Mr. Mack's offer, Salsinger suggested he pursue Cochrane. Salsinger advised Navin that Cochrane not only would solve his catching problem but that he also could provide the managerial leadership so badly needed in Detroit. Navin told his partner, Walter O. Briggs, who made his money manufacturing automobile parts, what he had in mind. Briggs loaned him $100,000 from his personal funds, and the Tigers were on their way to pennants in 1934 and 1935, and a world's championship in '35.

Navin made another deal shortly after acquiring Cochrane. He got veteran outfielder Goose Goslin from the Washington Senators for John (Rocky) Stone, another outfielder. Some felt it was an outright steal, that Navin must have sweetened the deal with a bundle of cash. But it was a straight-up swap, man for man. Though Goslin was 33 at the time, he was a true pro with plenty of baseball left in him. He was an instrumental figure in the

Bridgewater, Massachusetts-born Mickey Cochrane played four years and managed five in Detroit, but so endeared himself to the fans they named a narrow street behind the ballpark for him. ◆

Front row, third from right, sits the skipper of the 1934 American League champions, Mickey Cochrane. Along with the manager, three others—Charlie Gehringer, Goose Goslin, and Hank Greenberg are in the Hall of Fame. ◆

consecutive pennants, ultimately stroking the winning hit against the Chicago Cubs in the 1935 World Series.

A lot of things broke right for the Tigers in 1934. Lynwood "Schoolboy" Rowe, a 7–4 performer in 1933, became one of the most powerful pitchers in the league and ran up a 24–8 record. He won 16 in a row to tie a major league record. Best of all, he specialized in beating the Yankees. Tommy Bridges, a 14–12 performer the previous year, became a 22–11 star in '34. His curveball dazzled the entire league. Firpo Marberry finished 15–5 and Eldon Auker, the submarine pitcher, 15–7. Greenberg developed into a thunderous threat and good old Charlie Gehringer—Old Reliable—played with a steady brilliance that settled down the whole team. Cochrane was a firebrand behind the plate and the Tigers wound up with six players hitting .300 that season. Then they were all but run over by the St. Louis Cardinals in the World Series.

The St. Louis Gashouse Gang was a rollicking crew: The Dean brothers, Dizzy and Daffy; Joe Medwick, Frankie Frisch, and Pepper Martin. There was no stopping them.

The St. Louis team was a team of braggarts. They chided the long, lanky Greenberg by calling him "Moe," a derogatory reference to his Jewish background. Before the first game in De-

Eldon Auker ranked as the third Tiger starter on the pennant-winning '34 and '35 squads. He was noted for his distinctive "submarine" delivery. ◆

troit, Dizzy Dean went into the batting cage and said to Greenberg: "Hey, Moe, gimme that bat." He took the bat and drove the ball into the left field seats. "That's how you do it, Moe," Dean laughed.

When the two teams reached the seventh game in Detroit, tied at three games apiece, Dean seized the moment to torment the Tigers again. He showed up for practice with a tiger rug slung over his shoulders. He paraded in front of the stands and then walked in front of the Detroit dugout. He cried out, "I got me a Tiger skin already." When Auker started warming up for the Tigers, Dean called to Cochrane, "He won't do, Mickey!"

Final score: St Louis 11, Detroit 0.

This was the game that produced the famous "Medwick Incident": The St. Louis slugger had smashed a triple in the sixth

Joe Medwick put on a Brooklyn Dodger uniform in 1940. ♦

inning, and as he slid into third base, he tangled with third baseman Marvin Owen. The men bumped each other and stood nose to nose at the bag. Medwick was mad because Owen had duped him into thinking he had the ball, forcing Medwick to slide. Owen was irate because Medwick's spikes had nicked him on the slide. The Tigers trailed 9–0 at that point and the fans felt frustrated. When Medwick went to left field, he was met with a chorus of boos, followed by a shower of apples, tomatoes, oranges, peaches, pears, and banana skins, plus rolled up newspapers, and scorecards. Play had to be suspended.

Commissioner Kenesaw Mountain Landis, watching from a box seat behind third base, summoned Medwick from the field. He said Medwick would have to leave the game to keep order in the ballpark.

Frisch, the fire-spouting St. Louis player/manager, charged from his second base post to Landis' box.

"Why should I take him out!" he bellowed.

"Because I said so," Landis replied.

The commissioner was a tough bird and could not be easily intimidated. Besides, Pepper Martin had just taught him how to chew tobacco and spit out the juice, and the Judge was having too good a time to have his fun spoiled by some rowdy fans.

The following season, 1935, the Yankees dumped Babe Ruth, sending him to the Boston Braves in the National League where his career declined to an inglorious end. The Tigers weren't doing any better, themselves. They sank to last place at the end of April and as late as May 28, they had risen no higher than sixth. Their fans wondered if the success in 1934 had gone to their heads.

Slowly but surely, however, the Tigers pulled themselves together and started to climb in the standings. They took the lead in the middle of July from the Yankees and built up a nine-game margin, before finally winning by three games.

Greenberg had a great season. He was the most feared batter in the league. He batted .328 with 36 homers, 13 triples, 46 doubles, and 170 RBIs. After not being picked for the All-Star team, he was named the league's most valuable player. The All-Star voters had gone for Lou Gehrig and Jimmie Foxx at first base but there was no competition in the MVP balloting at the end of the season.

Gehringer hit a steady .330, and outfielder Pete Fox surprised everyone by batting .321; Cochrane, as bold and boisterous as ever, hit .319 and kept everyone hustling. Tommy Bridges was the pitching leader with a 21–10 mark, while Rowe was 19–13, Auker 18–7, and General Alvin Crowder 16–10.

Now came the business of trying to win a World Series.

"The dizziest, maddest, wildest and most exciting World Series game was interrupted by one of the wildest riots ever seen in a ball park in the sixth inning. For the first time that I know of, the crowd forced a manager to remove a player from the field. Twenty thousand people, massed aslant in the left field bleachers, turned into a deadly and vicious mob. Only a barrier of a steel screen and locked gates prevented them from pouring onto the field and mobbing outfielder Joe Medwick, who bears the innocuous nickname of Ducky Wucky."
    Paul Gallico, N.Y. *Daily News* ◆

Baseball Commissioner Kenesaw Mountain Landis, in attendance at the 1934 World Series, decided to remove Joe Medwick from the game for his own safety and so the game could proceed without further disturbance. ◆

The Chicago Cubs provided the opposition. Right away the breaks went against the Tigers when Greenberg collided with Chicago catcher Gabby Harnett in the second game and broke his wrist. He was finished for the rest of the Series.

The Tigers panicked. How do you replace a man of Greenberg's power? He had already slammed a home run before getting hurt in the game, helping Detroit to an 8–3 victory over the Cubs to square the Series at a game apiece.

Cochrane's first thought was to play first base himself and let Ray Hayworth, an old campaigner, handle the catching.

Navin listened to Cochrane's suggestion, then instructed him to move Marvin Owen from third to first and put the light-hitting Flea Clifton at third. Clifton was the weakest batter in the club, almost a sure out. When the players learned of the change, they went to Navin and complained. Navin stood firm. "If we lose the Series," he told them, "it'll be on my head." Clifton didn't get a hit in sixteen tries and Owen, playing a strange position, managed only one in 21 tries. But the Tigers didn't lose. Fox continued his fine hitting and so did Gehringer. Cochrane chipped in with some clutch hits, and Bridges and Crowder pitched well in the clutch.

Finally, on October 7, 1935, the Tigers became World Cham-

Tommy Bridges was a right-handed workhorse for the club in the middle of the Depression years. He was good for 22 victories in 1934 and followed up with 21 and a league-leading 23 in the next two years. ◆

S C R A P B O O K

"The A's arrived at Shibe Park for the opening game of 1925. . . . Came the eighth inning and the Red Sox had tied the score. . . . When it came Cy Perkins's turn to hit and Connie Mack commenced to look for a hitter . . . I remarked, 'Give me a bat, I can hit that guy.' . . . I went up and singled to left, driving in the winning run. Cy took off his catching equipment just as the man crossed the plate, the boys on the bench told me much later, and said, 'There goes Perkins's job on that base hit.' "

Mickey Cochrane

◆

"He [Cobb] treated me like he was my father; he sat with me on the trains and he told me all of the ways of hitting and the secrets of base running. . . . He made me use his own bat, which was a very thin-handled job and thin hitting space and I preferred something a little bigger, but he insisted that Heinie Manush and I would use his bat. And they were good bats, the best wood."

Charlie Gehringer, *Baseball for the Love of It*

◆

"Charlie [Gehringer] had a habit of taking the first pitch. We roomed together some when I was with the Tigers and I asked him once why he did it.

" 'So the pitcher can start off even with me,' he said."

Rudy York, *Sport*, 1953

◆

"As a fielder, Greenberg was an object lesson for every kid who has ever turned his face away from a hard ground ball. Because that's exactly what Hank used to do when he first came to the Tigers. But he *made* himself a good fielder. Even as a superstar, he was always the first one at the park. I know because more than once, three hours before game time, I was the only one in the stands watching him. Endlessly, he would hurl a ball against the outfield wall and field it on the hop, like a kid in his own backyard who has no one to play catch with." Art Hill, *I Don't Care If I Never Come Back*, Simon & Schuster, 1980

◆

"With the wind behind him [Schoolboy Rowe] he's pretty near as fast as my brother Paul."

Dizzy Dean before the 1934 World Series

◆

"I hadn't had a hit all day in that game, and when I came up to bat there in the ninth, with the score tied, two out and Mickey Cochrane on second, I said to the umpire, 'If they pitch that ball over this plate, you can go take that monkey suit off.'

"And sure enough, the first ball Larry French threw in there—zoom! Oh, did those Tiger fans ever go wild. I'll never forget it. I played with the Senators for twelve years, the Browns for two, and the Tigers for four, and the best baseball town I ever played in and for was Detroit. The fans there were great."

Goose Goslin to Lawrence Ritter, *The Glory of Their Times*

Happy fans gathered under the scoreboard at Navin Field after a ninth inning Tiger win in Game Six closed out the Series, 4–3. ◆

pions when they beat the Cubs 4–3 in the sixth game. They won it on Goose Goslin's ninth-inning single into right field, scoring Mickey Cochrane from second base. The fans danced in the streets and a night-long celebration ensued.

Store owners were fearful the fans would cave in their windows and phoned for police help. One group of revelers thought it would be fun to overturn a street car. The cops weren't the only people working overtime; the fire department was kept busy all night answering false alarms. The Depression was still at a peak, but these were happy days for the city of Detroit.

Celebrants in 1935 papered the streets of Detroit after the Mickey Cochrane–led Tigers recouped from the defeat of a year earlier. ♦

THE GREAT WAR—BEFORE AND AFTER

♦

I t was all over for Mickey Cochrane on May 15, 1937. That's when he was hit on the head by a ball and his playing career came to an end. Cochrane was a tough one—the spirit of the Tigers—but he had a difficult time controlling his own emotions. He got so wound up trying to beat the St. Louis Cardinals in the 1934 World Series that he checked himself into a hospital each night to get his proper rest. More than anything, he had wanted to get even with Pepper Martin, the reckless Cardinals base-runner who had made Cochrane look so bad in the 1931 World Series when Cochrane had been catching for Connie Mack's Philadelphia A's. Martin ran wild on the bases, stealing five times, and became known as the "Wild Horse of the Osage."

It wasn't much better in 1934. Martin stole only twice, but the Cardinals taunted Cochrane and his Tigers and finally closed them out with an 11–0 victory in the deciding game in Detroit. Two years later, in 1936, Cochrane suffered a nervous breakdown and was forced to leave the team. He went to a Wyoming ranch for an extended rest while coach Del Baker became interim manager. Cochrane returned by early August but caught very little, appearing in only forty-four games in the entire season. The Tigers, defending champions, finished 19½ games out of first place.

His fire died completely the following season.

That's when Cochrane was struck on the left temple by a pitch thrown by Bump Hadley of the Yankees. Cochrane threw up his hand to ward off the ball but it hit with a sickening thud on the side of his head. He collapsed to the ground, face first, unconscious. Rushed to a hospital, he was pronounced "critical" with

At the 1940 Series, Greenberg posed for a fan. He had finished the year with 40 homers, and a .340 average. Shortly after the 1941 season began he became the first major leaguer grabbed by the military draft. ♦

Playing manager Mickey Cochrane came to the Tigers in 1933 from the Philadelphia Athletics for $100,000 and Johnny Pasek, a second-string catcher. In 13 years the Hall of Famer hit .320, best ever of any receiver. The stress of managing after the pennant seasons of '34 and '35 drove him to a hospital and a leave of absence in 1936, and early in 1937 a pitch from Yankee Irving "Bump" Hadley skulled Cochrane, nearly killing him. He came back to manage, but could no longer do the job effectively. ◆

a triple skull fracture. Not until four days later were doctors able to determine that he would survive. But his playing days were over. Baker ran the team again until Cochrane returned on July 25. This time the Tigers finished 13 games out of first place.

Cochrane tried working with the Tigers strictly as a manager in 1938, but little went right for him. He tried to improve his pitching by dealing for Vern Kennedy, a 21-game winner with the White Sox. But he gave away Gee Walker, Marv Owen, and Mike Tresh in the process. These three were favorites in Detroit, and the fans got on Cochrane for the trade. As the club foundered, owner Walter O. Briggs became disenchanted with his manager. With the team in fifth place, Briggs summoned Cochrane to his office and fired him. The dismissal came a little more than a year after his beaning, and less than three years after Cochrane led the Tigers to the World's Championship. Del Baker took over as manager on a full-time basis.

Cochrane's departure seemed to signal the end of the happy days in Detroit, but the Tigers showed surprising strength in the war years, which were just on the horizon. No team in baseball was more colorful than the Tigers in those turbulent times from 1939 to 1945. They won two pennants—1940 and 1945—and also the World's Championship in 1945.

Both winning years were memorable.

The Tigers had finished 26½ games out of first place in 1939, and there was no reason to believe they would be a factor in 1940. The Yankees were clearly the dominant team in baseball. Led by their wondrous center fielder, Joe DiMaggio, the Yankees won four straight championships (1936–'37–'38–'39), and even though the mighty Lou Gehrig's career came to an end in 1939, the Yankees were favored to win again in 1940.

But Louis Norman (Bobo) Newsom had some other ideas.

Newsom was a big, bluff man. He looked like a buffalo. Or maybe a rhinoceros. Out on the mound he would snort and grunt and groan and sweat and strain whenever he let the ball go. He would twist and turn and come at you from over the top, from the side, underhanded, crossways, three-quarters, five-eighths, and his face would start turning crimson from all-out effort in the very first inning. He was a character, and the Tigers got him from the St. Louis Browns during the 1939 season.

Newsom was a courageous pitcher, but controversial. He couldn't keep his mouth shut. He thought he should be allowed to do things his way. The Browns dumped him after Newsom challenged the authority of manager Fred Haney, a firebrand himself.

One day when the Browns were being pushed around by the

Schoolboy Rowe, Hal Newhouser, and Tommy Bridges appeared on Old Timer's Day in 1958, having won a total of 499 games for the Tigers. ◆

Yankees, Newsom went to the bullpen and began warming up.

Haney said to him: "Who told you to warm up?"

"I did," replied Newsom. "I went down there in case you needed me."

"Well, I'm giving the orders around here," said Haney.

The St. Louis manager was fuming. One word led to another, and the two men began shouting at each other in the dugout.

The Tigers were the next team to play the Browns in Sportsman's Park and Tigers general manager Jack Zeller knew Newsom was available. He spent all day and part of the night trying to work out a trade with Brownie boss Bill DeWitt. They finally settled on a ten-man deal. Nobody knew it at the time, but getting Bobo Newsom was the start of the Tigers' success in 1940.

Living with this man was not easy. He called everybody "Bobo," and some of his conversations got a little ridiculous.

"Hey, Bobo."

"How are you, Bobo?"

"I'm fine, Bobo. How are you?"

"I'm good, Bobo."

Walter O. "Spike" Briggs was co-owner of the Tigers with Navin until Navin died in 1934. Briggs then bought his dead partner's shares and the Briggs family operated the club for twenty-five years. ◆

Norman Louis "Bobo" Newsom pitched the Tigers into the 1940 World Series with a spectacular 21–8 season, and he won a pair of Series contests as well. When he fell to 12–20 the following year, Detroit shipped him to the Senators for $40,000. Clark Griffith in Washington quickly tired of Newsom and that same year dished him off to Brooklyn for only $25,000. ♦

When Newsom was in St. Louis, owner Don Barnes promised him a new suit if he won the opening day game. Newsom came through, and Barnes went to the clubhouse after the game to give his pitcher the money.

"Don't worry about it," said Newsom.

"What do you mean—I promised you a new suit," said Barnes.

"I already bought it," said Newsom. "You'll find the bill on your desk."

Newsom was gifted with a rubber arm—he could pitch every day—and he had unshakeable confidence in himself. He felt he could beat anyone, anytime, anywhere. He was one tough old bird.

One time Earl Averill of the Indians smacked a line drive off Newsom's leg. Bobo picked himself up and pitched the final four innings. He walked into the clubhouse and announced to a startled trainer: "Bobo's laig is busted." It was, too—fractured just below the knee.

Another time, Newsom was struck by a thrown ball while starting an opening day game in Washington. He suffered a fractured jaw, but again wouldn't come out of the game.

"Are you crazy?" he said later on. "Come out of a game against the Yankees with the President of these United States sitting in the stands? Not old Bobo." Newsom won the game 1–0.

The big man became the heart of the Tigers in 1940. Zeller had made a lot of deals to bolster his club. He sent Billy Rogell to the Cubs for Dick Bartell in a trade of shortstops. Bartell became a sparkplug for the Tigers. Zeller traded Eldon Auker, Jake Wade, and Chet Morgan to the Boston Red Sox for Pinky Higgins and Archie McKain. Beau Bell was shipped to Cleveland for Bruce Campbell.

Zeller also talked Hank Greenberg into moving to the outfield to make room for the big Indian slugger, Rudy York, at first base. He gave Greenberg a $10,000 bonus to make the switch, raising

Mike "Pinky" Higgins shifted from the Red Sox to Detroit in 1939. His steady glove and hitting helped the Tigers win the pennant in 1940, and he hit .333 in a losing Series cause. ♦

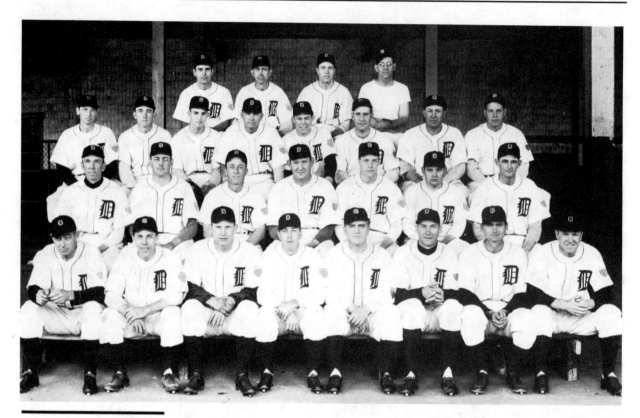

Steve O'Neill managed this 1945 Tiger band to the pennant and World Series. Missing from the portrait is Hank Greenberg, still in the U.S. Army Air Corps at the start of the season. Notables present include Rudy York, the first baseman who pushed Greenberg into the outfield and once hit 18 homers in one month (third row, second from right) and Paul Richards, who later devised the oversize catcher's mitt for handling knuckleballs, and managed the White Sox and Orioles (front row, second from right). ♦

High Henry's salary from $40,000 to $50,000. Greenberg worked hard to make himself a decent outfielder, and had a banner year at the plate in 1940. He batted .340, with 41 homers and 150 runs batted in. York thrived at first base with a .316 average, 33 homers, and 134 RBIs.

Newsom, though, was the leader. He won 21 games and lost only five, and never stopped talking. He was bragging about himself from the beginning of the season to the end. What made his record so remarkable is that he broke his thumb and was out for three weeks.

But before it all ended, pitcher Floyd Giebell had his moment in Cleveland.

The 1940 season was one of frustration for the Indians. It had started grandly with Bob Feller pitching a no-hitter on opening day in Chicago, but it quickly deteriorated into a very seamy scene in Cleveland.

The Indians had some solid players in Ben Chapman, Lou Boudreau, Ken Keltner, Mel Harder, and the fireballing Feller, but dissension set in on the club over the tactics of manager Oscar Vitt. The players drew up a petition to have him fired, and were branded "crybabies." It got so bad that when the Indians visited Detroit in the middle of the summer, the fans were dan-

Rudy York (left) broke in as a catching replacement for Mickey Cochrane in 1937 but was moved to first base, forcing Hank Greenberg into the outfield. York swung a potent bat, leading the league in homers in 1943 with 34 and a top slugging average of .527. Pitcher Floyd Giebell (right) threw a mere 28 innings for the club in three years of regular season play. But his clutch performance in 1940 helped the team fly a pennant. ◆

gling baby bottles—complete with nipples—in front of the Cleveland dugout.

The two teams fought all the way to a three-game series in Cleveland on the last weekend of the season. The Tigers were two games ahead, which meant they needed to win only one of the three games to clinch the pennant. The Indians needed a sweep to get a tie.

It was supposed to be Schoolboy Rowe against Bob Feller in a battle of aces in the opening game on Friday afternoon, but here was an unknown pitcher named Floyd Giebell warming up for the Tigers. He was a twenty-five-year-old right-hander just brought up from Buffalo. The Cleveland fans were confused. They didn't know what to make of the change.

Manager Del Baker had reasoned that since the Tigers needed only one more victory, they shouldn't waste one of their good pitchers against the almost unbeatable Feller. Baker offered his players a choice of having Hal Newhouser, Dizzy Trout, or Floyd Giebell pitch. Surprisingly, the players chose Giebell, who had no better than a 15–17 record in the International League. They were impressed with his composure. They felt he wouldn't get nervous in the big moment.

He didn't.

Giebell allowed only six hits and shut out the Indians 2–0 to wrap up the pennant. Feller allowed only three hits, but one of them was a two-run homer by York, a high fly which fell into the left field seats, barely fair, in the fourth inning.

The Yankees had struggled without Gehrig, their fabled "Iron Horse," and finished in third place, two games out.

Now it was Detroit against Cincinnati in the World Series and Bobo Newsom was ready.

In fact, he named himself to pitch the opener against the Reds.

"Who else but me?" Bobo said, laughing, as he spoke to the sportswriters.

Newsom was overpowering. He breezed past the Reds 7–2 and was never in any trouble after his teammates tagged Paul Derringer for five runs in the second inning. Game 1 was the biggest moment in Newsom's life, but he would soon suffer a most shattering blow.

Newsom's father had driven in from Hartsfield, South Carolina, with several members of the Newsom family, to see Bobo pitch the opener. Bobo had never been any prouder than he was winning before his folks from back home. That night they celebrated at the Netherlands Plaza Hotel in downtown Cincinnati. It was a gala occasion, but too much for the elder Newsom. He collapsed and died of a heart attack.

Many thought Bobo would not be seen again in the World Series, but after his father was buried, he came back and, with tears in his eyes, shut out the Reds 8–0 on three hits in Game 5 in Detroit. That gave the Tigers a three-to-two lead as the Series switched back to Cincinnati.

As in 1934, Schoolboy Rowe was given the task of wrapping up the World Series for the Tigers. Again, he failed. He retired only one batter and was removed when the Reds got to him for two runs in the first inning. Rowe hurt himself by forgetting to cover first base on a close play. The Reds went on to a 4–0 victory.

That left it up to Louis Norman Newsom—who else?—to start Game No. 7. Again his opponent was Paul Derringer. Working with just one day of rest, Newsom had the Reds blanked 1–0 in the seventh inning, when his dream ended. The Reds pushed over two runs as Newsom was the victim of a fielding mistake.

Frank McCormick started the seventh with a double to the wall in left. Jimmie Ripple followed with another two-bagger; this one hit the top of the right field screen. McCormick thought the ball might be caught and hesitated between second and third. He stopped again rounding third base. Bruce Campbell fielded the ball and threw it in to shortstop Dick Bartell. Bartell made no play on McCormick at the plate. In fact, he didn't even turn around, even though his teammates implored him to throw home. Motion pictures later disclosed that Bartell would have had a chance to get McCormick. But the damage was done. The Reds got the deciding run when Ripple moved over to third and scored on a sacrifice fly.

Fred Hutchinson pitched his entire major league career in Detroit, from his rookie year of 1939 to the final few innings of 1953, with five years out for wartime service. He was that rare specimen, the pitcher-manager, in '52 and '53 with the Tigers. ◆

George "Birdie" Tebbetts was the catcher who gradually took over after Cochrane was beaned in 1937. ♦

It was Cincinnatti 2, Detroit 1.

Newsom was visibly upset after the game. A reporter went to him and asked him how he felt.

"I feel terrible," said Newsom. "I really wanted this one."

"For your dad?" asked the reporter.

"Naw," said Newsom, grinning. "I wanted this one for Bobo."

The glow of winning the pennant didn't last long for the Tigers. Newsom slumped to a 12–20 record in 1941, and the front office slashed his salary from $34,000 to $12,500. They could do those things in those days.

The war in Europe was on and on May 17, just 19 games into the season, Hank Greenberg, strong and single, became the first American Leaguer to be drafted into the Army. He went willingly, but the fans were unhappy. They did not want to lose their big slugger, especially since the U.S. was not at war with anyone.

Outfielder Barney Mc-Cosky hit better than .300 over his four-plus seasons with the Tigers, but he's best recalled in Detroit as the player swapped to the Philadelphia Athletics in 1946 for the incomparable George Kell, who was only a promising newcomer at that point. ♦

The Tigers finished fifth, 26 games out, and conditions didn't get any better as the war clouds gathered over Detroit, the most industrialized city in the land.

When the Japanese struck Pearl Harbor, Tigers owner Walter O. Briggs stopped making automobiles and began producing tanks. He had purchased the steel to erect light towers atop his ballpark—now known as Briggs Stadium—but when the war broke out, he cancelled the order and donated the steel to his country. With the war plants going around the clock, interest in the Tigers fell off in 1942. Attendance slumped to a ten-year low of 580,000. The Tigers finished fifth, 30 games out of first place.

Jack Zeller, the general manager, fed up with Newsom, sold him to Washington. After nearly three seasons with Detroit, Newsom was 35 and considered finished. He would, however, last ten more years—until the 1953 season, making seventeen stops in his amazing twenty-year career.

The call to arms continued in 1943 with the likes of Charlie Gehringer, Barney McCoskey, Pat Mullin, Birdie Tebbetts, Al Benton, and Freddie Hutchinson being summoned to service. Steve O'Neill replaced Del Baker as manager. Some players received 4-F exemptions to work in war plants but they were a minority. With the plants operating full-time, the Tigers scheduled some of the games at five and six o'clock in the afternoon, calling them twilighters. They never caught on.

A restriction on train travel forced the Tigers to hold their spring training camp in Evansville, Indiana, a cold and wet place in the month of March. It was almost impossible to line up any exhibition games, so Jack Zeller hatched the idea of having his players pack up their gear and hike to the camp of the Chicago White Sox in Terre Haute—a mere 112 miles away.

Zeller said to O'Neill, "A lot of young men are carrying packs these days. Our guys will only have to carry their bats, balls, and gloves. You could stop five or six times along the way."

O'Neill said to his boss, "If they walk, they'll have to do it without their manager."

The quality of the game suffered badly during the war. President Franklin D. Roosevelt decreed that baseball should continue because it would boost the morale of the factory workers. Some teams along the eastern seaboard were not allowed to play at night for fear the light from their giant towers would illuminate the Atlantic Ocean and make it easier for German U-boats to prey on Allied shipping.

The Tigers created history of a sort in 1943 by making outfielder Dick Wakefield the first bonus player in the history of

baseball. They signed him out of the University of Michigan for $55,000. He batted .316, getting 200 hits in his rookie year in 1943. Drafted the following year, he was granted a 90-day leave before going into service in 1944. Even though he did not get enough at bats to qualify for the batting title, Wakefield batted .355 in 1944 and the Tigers missed out on the pennant that year by one game. When he came out of service, Wakefield never regained his wartime form.

Baseball had become something of a bad joke by the end of the war. The game was being played by a ragtag collection of players. The St. Louis Browns used a courageous one-armed outfielder named Pete Gray. The Yankee catcher, Mike Garbark, went hitless in 49 straight trips to the plate and when he finally smacked a double, he leaned down and hugged second base.

Happy Chandler was the new commissioner of baseball in 1944, having succeeded Judge Kenesaw Mountain Landis, who had died the year before. Chandler was like a king without a castle. He ruled over a wasteland of mediocrity. The Tigers got 29 victories from Hal Newhouser and 27 from Dizzy Trout, and nearly won the pennant. They lost out on the final day, splitting a doubleheader with Washington while the Browns were sweeping a pair from the Yankees.

Washington finished the 1945 season with an 87–67 record. Their season ended a week before everyone else's because the Senators' owner, Clark Griffith, a man totally committed to the dollar, wanted to rent the ballpark to the Washington Redskins football team.

Hank Greenberg, discharged as a captain shortly after V-E Day, powered the club to the pennant with some late-season heroics, hitting 13 homers and compiling 60 RBIs in 78 games. With manager Steve O'Neill, he greeted some of the recent civilians in the stands before the World Series. ◆

"Prince Hal" Newhouser grew up in Detroit and over the years the slender lefty pitched his hometown to an even 200 wins. ◆

Hank Greenberg misses a bad pitch in the 1945 World Series. ◆

All the Senators could do was sit and wait for the outcome of the Detroit games. The Tigers went into the last two days in St. Louis with an 87–65 record. If they won one game, the pennant would be theirs; if they lost both games, it would be a tie, with a one-game playoff set in Detroit for the following Monday.

The next-to-last game was set for a Saturday afternoon, but it was rained out. A doubleheader was scheduled on Sunday. When the teams got to Sportman's Park on Sunday morning, the field was almost a swamp. The ground was soft and mushy. As the groundskeepers worked to make the field in St. Louis playable, four men were huddled around a radio in a hotel room in downtown Detroit to listen to the St. Louis games. They were pitchers Dutch Leonard, Walter Masterson, Roger Wolfe, and Mickey Haefner of the Senators. They had been sent to Detroit in anticipation of a one-game playoff on Monday, October 1.

Back in Washington, meanwhile, the rest of the Senators gathered in the clubhouse at Griffith Stadium. They had their bags packed, ready to take the 5:10 P.M. train to Detroit. When the Browns edged ahead by a run in the eighth inning of the

first game, the players began getting ready to board the bus to the train terminal.

"We thought surely there would be a game on Monday," recalled catcher Rick Ferrell.

In St. Louis—with a steady drizzle falling—the Tigers loaded the bases in the ninth inning and Greenberg came up against Nelson Potter, ace of the St. Louis staff. The players' vision was hampered by the rain, but Greenberg connected and belted a line drive toward the left field bleachers. The ball was barely fair, clearing the wall at the 351-foot marker. Pandemonium broke out in the Detroit dugout. The big guy—Hankus Pankus, the first American Leaguer in the military and among the first demobilized—had come back to save them all. The Tigers had won the pennant. The umpires called off the second game.

In Detroit, the four Washington players clicked off the radio and made plans to return to Washington. In Washington, the players got off the bus and returned to their homes.

Outside the Telenews Theater on Woodward Avenue in Detroit, where the game was being piped into the streets, the people began going wild. Fearing they would start tearing up the theater, the owner cried out: "Quick, put on the National Anthem before they get out of hand!"

All of which brings us to Chuck Hostetler.

If any one player embodied all that wartime baseball was about, it was outfielder Chuck Hostetler of the Tigers. The Tigers played the Cubs in the World Series and both teams were so weak—their rosters so depleted—that columnist Warren Brown of the *Chicago American* wrote: "This is one World Series that neither team can win."

He was almost right. The two sides took turns at winning, with neither showing very much style. They bottomed out in the sixth game in Wrigley Field in Chicago. Each team used nineteen players—thirty-eight in all—and the game lasted three hours and thirty-eight minutes, a long time in those days, before the Cubs finally won 8–7 and squared the series at three games apiece. If they'd won this game, the Tigers could have clinched it. But Hostetler took a pratfall between third and home.

With the Tigers trailing 5–1 in the seventh inning, Hostetler was on second base when Roger Cramer shot a single into left field. Hostetler took off. He headed for third base, where manager Steve O'Neill was handling the coaching duties. O'Neill held up his hands for Hostetler to stop. Good old Chuck kept right on going. He rounded third and was more than halfway home when he decided to put on the brakes. He went down to the ground, bouncing along on all fours. It was a simple matter for the Cubs

Paul "Dizzy" Trout had a reputation as an ornery pitcher and would throw at anybody who crowded "his" plate, even icons like Joe Di-Maggio. He won 151 games in a Tiger suit. But when Tommy Henrich was playing his final game for the Yankees before entering the Coast Guard in 1942, Trout threw Tommy six straight fastballs—Henrich feasted on fast-balls—to give him his best chance for a hit. ◆

to tag him out. The Tigers went on to score two runs in the inning and four more in the eighth to tie it up. If Hostetler had scored, or held up—or done anything at all but land on his face—the Tigers could have won in regulation time.

Frank Graham, a kindly sports writer from New York City, called it "the worst game ever played in a World Series. It was the fat men against the skinny men at an office picnic."

Even when the Cubs pushed over the deciding run in the twelfth inning, it was not without great controversy—not over the run, but over how it was scored. The Cubs won when a ball shot past Greenberg in left field and precipitated an official scoring debacle.

With Bill Schuster on first base, Stan Hack of the Cubs lined a ball into left field. Greenberg went down to field it but the ball hopped past him and rolled to the ivy-covered wall. Schuster scored all the way from first base with the winning run. There were three official scorers in the press box: H. G. Salsinger, Mike Haley, and Ed Burns. They agreed to call it a single for Hack and two-base error by Greenberg, allowing Schuster to score.

Greenberg was so mad at the decision he would not talk to any of the reporters after the game. He insisted the ball had hit a drainpipe, causing it to jump over his shoulder. There was such a furor over the call that other writers covering the World Series met that night with Haley and Burns at the Palmer House hotel and protested the decision. The two men decided to change their call. They would award Hack a two-base hit, with no error on Greenberg, and Schuster scoring on the double. They called Salsinger in his room. Sal said, "Do what you like—I'm going to sleep." The scoring change occurred too late for the morning

Best remembered for a pratfall while rounding third base in the 1945 World Series, Chuck Hostetler was a 30-year-old rookie when he came to the bigs. ◆

Pitcher Hal Newhouser, a 25-game winner in 1945, glumly watches Don Johnson score the first of eight runs he yielded in the opening game of the Series against the Chicago Cubs. Newhouser recovered to win Games 5 and 7 for a Tiger world championship. ◆

S C R A P B O O K

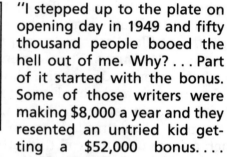

"Rudolph Preston York, the muscular house painter of Cartersville, Georgia, was a large copper-colored man with about three fingers of Cherokee blood in his veins. 'Rudy York,' wrote the late Tom Meany, 'part Indian and part first baseman . . .'

"Rudy York was an outfielder, a third baseman, and a catcher as well as a first baseman. . . . No matter where he was stationed in the field, Rudy York always played the same position.

"He played bat.

"He was slow, unskilled, awkward, sincere, tireless, and stronger than dirt. There were many things he couldn't do well on a playground and some he couldn't do at all but when he swung a bolt of mountain ash, the baseball left the neighborhood . . .

Red Smith, *Women's Wear Daily*, 1970

◆

"To [Steve O'Neill] this tough-looking, muffin-faced old catcher out of the anthracite mines of Minooka, Pennsylvania, Einstein and e.e. cummings and the Bolshoi Ballet were strictly for the birds, but he could sniff out baseball talent in the heaviest cover and he had a rare knack for keeping players relaxed. . . .

"In thirteen seasons as a manager in the big leagues Steve had only one pennant winner. That was the Detroit club of 1945, which beat the Cubs in a World Series witnessed by the largest and most horrified crowds any Series had drawn up to then. 'The richest of all World Series' it was called 'and the poorest.' "

Red Smith, *New York Herald Tribune*, 1962

"I stepped up to the plate on opening day in 1949 and fifty thousand people booed the hell out of me. Why? . . . Part of it started with the bonus. Some of those writers were making $8,000 a year and they resented an untried kid getting a $52,000 bonus. . . . Greenberg—the star of the team—was only making around $40,000 a year. Who the hell is Wakefield? But *Greenberg* didn't care how much money I'd gotten. Hank didn't give a damn. More power to you kid—that's the way he felt about it."

Dick Wakefield to Donald Honig, *Baseball Between the Lines*

◆

"Cochrane and Dickey [Bill, catcher for the New York Yankees] were two of the finest catchers in the league at that time and of course he [Cochrane] was a good hitter, not a distance hitter, but he put the ball in play. As a manager he was very good, very good. He was a tough loser and he made you fight even though you were behind 10–1. And boy, if he lost on an error and maybe the guy played it carelessly he would stare at you and you'd know that he wouldn't have to say anything.

"After he got hit in the head, it seemed like he made more mistakes calling from the bench than he did when he was right in the action. He didn't seem like he ever made a mistake on anything—changing pitchers, doing anything when he was catching because he was so close to everything."

Charlie Gehringer to Rod Roberts, 1985

newspapers and the nation awoke the next day believing Greenberg's error had cost the game. Movies later showed that the ball did indeed hit a drainpipe and bounce past Greenberg.

The final game was almost anticlimactic. The Tigers scored five runs in the first inning when Paul Richards, their light-hitting catcher, cleared the bases with a double into the left field corner. The Tigers won 9–3.

That's not what people remember, however. Whenever anyone brings up the 1945 World Series, the response usually is: "Wasn't that the year Chuck Hostetler fell on his face rounding third . . .?"

THE POST-WAR YEARS

◆

After their war-tainted victory in 1945, it would take the Tigers twenty-three years—until 1968—before they would finish on top again. Even though they struggled through much of this time, it was anything but a dull period for baseball in Detroit.

- They would put lights in their ballpark in 1948—the last team in the American League to do so.
- They would see one of their players win a batting title on the final play of the season.
- They would play against a midget.
- They would get two no-hitters in one season—by the same pitcher.
- They would finish last for the first time in history.
- They would trade a batting champion for a home run champion.
- They would trade managers.
- They would use three managers in one season, with two of them dying.
- They would lose a pennant on the last play of the season.

The period from 1945 through 1968 was important to the Tigers because that was when they would put in place the management team which would lead them to championships in 1968 and 1984.

When you think of Detroit baseball after World War II, you think of such players as Hal Newhouser, George Kell, Vic Wertz, Johnny Groth, Hoot Evers, Dizzy Trout, Virgil Trucks and, of course, catcher Aaron Robinson, who got confused and forgot to tag the runner at home plate in a game in Cleveland and hurt the Tigers' chances of winning a pennant in 1950.

Bad wheels hobbled George Kell but nevertheless he topped American League third sackers in fielding percentage seven times, four times in assists and putouts, and twice in double plays. ◆

It was an exciting period in Detroit. The factories were producing cars again, and as they rolled off the assembly lines, the good times returned to the Motor City. The fans took to the postwar Tigers, flocking to the ballpark in record numbers. The fans especially liked the lights, even if the ball club didn't know how to use them in the beginning.

When the Tigers played their first night game on June 15, 1948, the management didn't think the lights would take effect until it got dark, so they delayed the start of the game until 9:30 P.M. Since the gates opened at 6 P.M., there was little for the fans to do for the next three and a half hours but sit there and look at the grass. They were rewarded for their patience with a 4–1 victory over the Philadelphia A's, with Prince Hal Newhouser handling the pitching.

George Trautman was the general manager of the Tigers in 1946 and made one of the best trades in the history of the club. With one month gone in the season, he got third baseman George Kell from the Philadelphia A's for outfielder Barney McCosky. Kell, who had been cut loose by the Brooklyn Dodgers organization before signing on with Connie Mack in Philadelphia, became an immediate fixture on the Tigers. He became the premier third baseman in the American League. He had weak knees—a malady from childhood—but was surprisingly agile on the bases. A tough fielder, he challenged every ball and at the plate he would drive the pitchers to distraction by changing his place in the batter's box on almost every pitch. He hit better than .300 in

"Al Kaline was with the Tigers for twenty-two years, and he played on a lot of bad teams, but he did not lower his standards to fit the company. . . . He was born a star; he made himself a superstar."

—Art Hill, *I Don't Care If I Never Come Back*

his first seven seasons in Detroit, but no year was more mean-ingful—or more challenging—than when he beat out Ted Williams for the batting championship on the final day of the 1949 season. Kell won it by two ten-thousandths of a percentage point—.3429 to .3427.

"We fought it out all through September, but whoever thought of beating out Ted Williams for anything?" Kell recalled. "We went into the final day and I was two points behind him and didn't give myself much of a chance."

As Kell was getting into uniform before the game, Hoot Evers said to him: "You know something—you're going to win this thing."

Kell looked at him. "No way," he said.

Williams was in New York, closing out the season with the Boston Red Sox. The Sox were in a flat-footed tie for first place with the Yankees and the game would decide the pennant. The Tigers were finishing up at home against the Cleveland Indians. All that was at stake was third place . . . and an outside chance for the batting title.

"I figured Williams would really be up for his game and with that short right field fence in Yankee Stadium, I thought he

Armed with a bat, George Kell (left) never dipped below .300 during his seven seasons in Detroit (five full ones, two partials). In 1952, Virgil Trucks (right) won five and lost 19, hurling a pair of no-hitters. Teammate Art Houtteman dropped 20 decisions as the club finished last for the first time in its history. ♦

might have a big day for himself," said Kell. "We were closing out against Bob Lemon and he was one of the toughest pitchers I'd ever faced in my life."

Kell singled and doubled in his first two trips against Lemon. The Indians brought in Bob Feller and Kell struck out against him in his third trip to the plate.

Meanwhile, word came in from New York that the Yankees had beaten Boston 5—0 and Williams had gone hitless in two trips. Lyall Smith, sports editor of the *Detroit Free Press*, did some quick calculating in the press box. He discovered if Kell didn't go to the plate again, he would be the batting champion. Word was relayed to the Detroit dugout.

The Tigers, trailing in the game, were coming to bat in the ninth and Kell was scheduled to be the fourth hitter. Johnny Lipon, a pinch-hitter, began the ninth by grounding out. Dick Wakefield batted for pitcher Hal White and singled. As Eddie Lake, the light-hitting shortstop, made his way to the plate, manager Red Rolfe said to Kell, "What do you want to do? Do you want to hit or do you want me to use somebody for you?"

Kell paused for a moment. "I'll hit," he said. He didn't want to back into the batting championship.

As Kell started for the on-deck circle, Lake swung at the first pitch and hit a ground ball to Ray Boone at shortstop. Boone fielded the ball near second base, stepped on the bag, and threw to first for a game-ending double play. Kell let out a yell and tossed his bat in the air.

The post-war team, a perennial contender, finally fell apart, and by 1952 the Tigers were in deep trouble. They finished last for the first time in their history, 45 games behind the Yankees. That same year, Virgil Trucks pitched two no-hitters, even though his record was no better than 5—19. He also threw a one-hitter, giving up a single to Eddie Yost of the Washington Senators on the first pitch of the game and then retiring 27 batters in a row.

The drama began on April 26, 1952. That's when Art Houtteman went to the mound for the Tigers in a game against the Cleveland Indians in Detroit. He had a no-hitter with two out in the ninth, when Harry (Suitcase) Simpson lined a sharp single into left field.

Three weeks later—on May 15—Detroit pitcher Virgil Trucks was getting ready to face the Washington Senators in Detroit. But he had a problem. His feet were hurting. He couldn't get into his spikes.

"Here, use my shoes," said Houtteman in the clubhouse. "They're a little bigger."

Harvey Kuenn pivots for the double play against the Yankees. A shortstop at the dawn of his career, Kuenn led the league in hits in his second and third years as a major leaguer. His best average of .353 in 1958 came while he was an outfielder and after he "slumped" to .308 the club traded him to Cleveland for Rocky Colavito, a deal that infuriated fans in both cities. ◆

The Tigers thought Vic Wertz could supply the punch once delivered by Hank Greenberg. In 1949 he drove across 133 runs, and the following year only slightly fewer, 123. When his stats slipped, the club dished him off to St. Louis, which subsequently traded him to Cleveland. Playing in the 1954 World Series with the Indians, he had the dubious distinction of hitting a tremendous fly ball for a spectacular catch by New York Giant Willie Mays at the Polo Grounds. ◆

They were the same spikes Houtteman wore the day he lost his no-hitter with two out in the ninth.

Trucks didn't think anything of it. He went out and held the Senators hitless through nine innings. The score was 0–0 when the Tigers came up in the bottom of the ninth.

Only 2,215 were in the ballpark. Most of the folks were lining the streets of downtown Detroit for a parade in honor of General Douglas MacArthur. Too bad . . . because they missed a very dramatic moment.

When the first two batters went out for the Tigers, Trucks sat in the dugout thinking about the time he'd thrown a nine-inning no-hitter at Buffalo in the International League and lost it, plus the game, with two out in the tenth.

Now, Vic Wertz was the batter. Wertz had doubled off Washington pitcher Bob Porterfield in the seventh inning. At that time he'd been the potential run that could have put Trucks into the lead, but Wertz was ignominiously picked off second base.

A lefthanded slugger, Wertz knew how to reach the short porch in right. He swung at Porterfield's first pitch and the ball started rising toward the right field stands. It crashed against the seats in the upper deck and Trucks leaped from the bench, hitting his head against the roof of the dugout. Even though he was dazed, he bolted onto the field and was the first player to greet Wertz at the plate. Catcher Joe Ginsberg was out there, too, even though he had strapped on his shin guards and chest protector in preparation for the tenth inning.

If this no-hitter seemed a little zany, you should have been around for the next one three months later—on August 25 in Yankee Stadium. Things got outright loony.

Trucks, a 33-year-old righthander, was credited with his second no-hitter when the official scorer changed his mind—not once, but twice—on a play in the third inning.

Phil Rizzuto of the Yankees bounded a ball toward shortstop Johnny Pesky. Pesky appeared to field the ball cleanly but juggled it while pulling it from his glove. When he made his throw to first base, it was low and late. John Drebinger, the official scorer from the *New York Times*, immediately ruled it an error. Then, after a moment of hesitation—deciding the ball had stuck in Pesky's glove—he changed it to a hit. The other writers in the press box protested. They felt it should have been an error. Drebinger held his ground— at least until the fifth inning. He was getting so much heat from his colleagues, he began to wonder if he had made the wrong call. He mulled it over and as the Tigers were coming to the plate in the seventh inning, he called the Detroit dugout and asked if he could speak to Pesky. Pesky told him he should have made the play.

"I messed up," said Pesky. "I should have had the ball, but it squirted from my grasp as I pulled it from my glove."

At this precise moment, the Tigers were breaking a scoreless tie on a double by Walt Dropo and a single by Steve Souchock.

Drebinger reversed his call and went back to his original ruling of an error. When the scoreboard reverted to "Yankees 0–0–0," the fans let out a cheer. They, too, thought it was an error by Pesky.

One person who didn't like the ruling was sitting in the Yankee dugout. He started screaming almost immediately. Manager Casey Stengel did not want his team to suffer the indignity of a no-hitter.

Trucks put the Yankees down in order in the seventh and eighth innings, while Stengel was storming up and down the dugout.

Mickey Mantle led off the ninth. "You can hit this busher!" Stengel cried out to him.

Mantle struck out.

Joe Collins was next. He was the clutch-hitting first baseman of the Yankees.

"Just poke the ball . . . just drive it over the infield!" Stengel yelled.

Collins lifted a long fly to right center, which Johnny Groth took on the run.

Now it was up to Hank Bauer, the grizzled veteran of the Yankees. "Lucky . . . plain lucky," Stengel was stewing. "This guy can't get by with no hits. I don't believe it."

Bauer hit a hard grounder but it went straight to second baseman Al Federoff. He took it on one bounce and threw Bauer out easily. The fans in New York stood and applauded Trucks as he walked off the field. He doffed his cap back to them. Four months later he was traded to the St. Louis Browns.

A skinny young outfielder—the son of a Baltimore broommaker—would make his appearance in Detroit the following summer. In 1955, in his second full season, Al Kaline would become the American League's youngest batting champion with a .340 average at the age of 20. He would give the Tigers 22 years of excellence—brilliant fielding in right and sound hitting at the plate. Kaline earned a place in the Hall of Fame with other Detroit greats Ty Cobb, Sam Crawford, Hughie Jennings, Harry Heilmann, Mickey Cochrane, Hank Greenberg, Charlie Gehringer, Goose Goslin, and George Kell.

Even with the emergence of Kaline as a star in the American League, the Tigers struggled through the rest of the 1950s, before making some sensational news in 1960. As the team was

From an awkward-swinging nineteen-year-old rookie in 1953, Kaline blossomed into a premier outfielder and outstanding hitter. When he finally laid down his bat he picked up the microphone to become an articulate and honest voice of the Tigers. ◆

The 1959 Tiger chaw champs were Harvey Kuenn (left) and Rocky Bridges, the itinerant infielder (center). Al Kaline was a gum man, himself. ◆

preparing to break camp in Lakeland, Florida, the Detroit management dropped a bombshell by announcing it had traded batting champion Harvey Kuenn (.353 in 1959) to the Cleveland Indians for home run king Rocky Colavito (42 homers in 1959). It was the first time a batting champion had been exchanged for a home run champion. The deal was made by two bold individuals—Bill DeWitt, who had been placed in charge of the Detroit front office, and Frank (Trader) Lane, the wheeler-dealer who was running the show in Cleveland. These two loved to draw attention to themselves and, in August of 1960, they outdid the Kuenn-Colavito swap by arranging the first—and only—trade of managers: Jimmie Dykes for Joe Gordon. Dykes lasted a year and a half in Cleveland but Gordon took one long, horrified look at the Tigers and shook his head. When the remainder of the season was over, he barricaded himself in his apartment and refused to talk to anyone. He quit.

Lane, meanwhile, had infuriated all of Cleveland by dealing away Colavito. The Rock was the idol of the fans—especially the young female fans. They threatened to boycott the ballpark.

"What's all the fuss about?" chortled Lane. "All I did was trade a hamburger for a steak."

That did it. The irate fans showed up with ropes, ready to string the Cleveland G.M. up on the nearest lamppost. Lane was ecstatic with the reaction—especially when the two teams opened the season in Cleveland and Colavito went hitless in six tries for the Tigers, striking out four times, popping up, and hitting into a double play.

A few years later, the Tigers had more problems with their managers. Serious problems. Charley Dressen, in his second full season in 1965, suffered a heart attack in spring training and was replaced for the twelve weeks he was in the hospital by coach Bob Swift. History sadly repeated itself in 1966. On May 16, Dressen suffered another heart attack, compounded by a kidney malfunction, and he died on August 10. Swift took Dressen's place again but his tenure also was brief. He was diagnosed as suffering from lung cancer and was relieved by Frank Skaff midway through the season. Swift died on October 17.

A year later, in 1967, the city of Detroit burned from the riot and the Tigers were beaten out for the pennant on the last day of the season. In fact, they lost when the final batter, Dick McAuliffe, hit into a season-ending double play.

These were tumultuous times for the Tigers, but smack in the middle of them, the Tigers would find the man who would

The biggest Tiger guns were Rocky Colavito (left), Al Kaline (center), and Norm Cash. Colavito in his four seasons with the team hit 139 homers, Cash amassed 373 in fifteen years, and Kaline had 399 over twenty-two campaigns. ◆

In 1956 Spike Briggs joined catcher Frank "Pig" House, and pitchers Virgil Trucks and Ned Garver in the sun. When the club wound up fifth, House, Trucks, and Garver all went to Kansas City in trades. It didn't help that much. The 1957 club only moved up one notch. ◆

bring stability to their organization. His name was John E. Fetzer, and he headed up a syndicate which bought the team in 1956.

In effect, the Tigers had had only two owners until Fetzer came along—Frank Navin, who purchased the club in the early 1900s from William Yawkey and took it to the middle 1930s, and Walter O. Briggs, who assumed control after Navin died in 1935. The Briggs family was in charge until 1956, when it was decreed that the ball club was not a "prudent" investment for the trust funds set up for the minor heirs of the Briggs estate. The club was ordered to be sold.

It was at this point that John E. Fetzer—good, gray John, who never raised his voice and preferred to remain in the background—became the new owner of the Detroit baseball club.

Fetzer, a radio-TV executive from Kalamazoo, Michigan, came along at the most complex time of all. Baseball was expanding on all fronts—financially, geographically, and even philosophically. The game was coming into the modern age—an age to be ruled by television, something which Fetzer understood quite clearly.

In the middle 1950s, baseball was in a struggle with pro football for the entertainment dollar. Pro football was gradually winning. The game fit almost perfectly into the TV screens, while the violence of the sport was embraced by a nation which fed on violence during the turbulent 1960s. It was a time of racial problems, campus unrest, street riots, and internal strife which took the lives of John F. Kennedy, Robert Kennedy, and Martin Luther King, Jr.

The game of baseball was further weakened by expansion, which resulted in a dilution of talent. As an astute businessman, Fetzer brought stability to the chaotic situation in Detroit and, at the same time, promoted a national television package which helped all the major league teams.

But it took some slick work by good, gray John to gain possession of the club.

He had to do a number on another savvy operator, Bill Veeck.

The last thing Fetzer wanted was to buy himself a ball club. Baseball was not his game. But some of his friends came to him and said they were interested in forming a syndicate to buy the Tigers but didn't know how to go about doing it. Without considering the consequences, Fetzer said he would help them.

Seven groups were preparing bids to purchase the ball club. One of them was headed by Bill Veeck, the flamboyant former impresario of the Cleveland Indians and St. Louis Browns.

The ground rules specified that all bids should be sealed and placed in the mail by midnight, July 2, 1956.

Veeck was the name everyone knew—the man everyone was watching. He discussed freely how he would revive the decaying franchise in Detroit. He would bring in clowns and shoot off fireworks and install an exploding scoreboard. That would wake them up.

Detroit didn't seem ready for such drastic changes. At least the old patriarch, H. G. Salsinger of the *Detroit News*, wasn't ready. Sal had covered the Tigers for more than fifty years and did not want to see it turned into a three-ring circus. He had suffered a cruel injury on opening day in 1954. He was in his seventies, a frail man who moved about slowly, and he was sitting in the press box in Briggs Stadium as the Baltimore Orioles— the St. Louis Browns the year before—were playing their first game in the American League since 1952. Steve Gromek, the Detroit starter, hit a foul ball into the press deck up near the roof and it struck Salsinger in the face. He was knocked off his seat and went into a state of shock. The ball struck his eye and cost him his vision in that eye. It was the last time Sal would ever be in the ballpark.

But now, in 1956, he decided to speak out one more time about his beloved Tigers.

Clowns? Fireworks? Exploding scoreboards? Not if old Sal could help it. He wrote a scathing editorial imploring the Tigers not to sell to this huckster, this medicine man with his traveling

John Fetzer gained control of the club after the death of Spike Briggs forced the estate to surrender its stock in 1956, and he became principal owner in 1961. A believer in one-man control rather than group proprietorship, Fetzer picked Tom Monaghan as the best man to succeed him. He remains chairman of the board. ♦

Jim Campbell, President and Chief Executive Officer of the Tigers, has been with the team for forty years, his entire career in baseball. Campbell is credited with developing the teams that won the World Series in 1968 and 1984. He hired Sparky Anderson to manage in 1979. ◆

show. It was very powerful prose from a highly respected source and many felt it cost Veeck his chance to buy the ball club.

Salsinger's words had nothing to do with it.

A shrewd maneuver by Fetzer did.

The Fetzer group felt the winning bid would range between four and five million dollars. In setting up their own financial structure, the Fetzer group obtained a two millon dollar line of credit from the National Bank of Detroit.

Meanwhile, Veeck was sounding off in the papers, detailing the financial structure of his bid and indicating that the National Bank of Detroit had extended his syndicate a line of credit up to two and a half million dollars.

Fetzer and his group had been prepared to bid $4.8 million, but Fetzer read Veeck's comments in the paper, and guessed that the bank had asked Veeck to match the credit line with an equal amount of money—putting his bid at $5 million.

Fetzer hastily called his colleagues together—not an easy task since there were eleven men in the syndicate. He detailed the problem to them. He figured they were $200,000 below Veeck's bid. It was only a guess, but he suggested they raise their bid to $5.5 million or retire from the contest. They went along with him and upped the ante.

On July 3, the sealed bids were opened at a formal board meeting of the Detroit Baseball Company. Veeck's bid was $5.2 million. All the others were less. Fetzer had guessed right.

Veeck was angry. He cried foul. He felt he had been slickered somewhere along the way. The finger pointed to H. G. Salsinger. It should have pointed at John E. Fetzer.

Veeck was so upset he verbally raised his bid to $6 million. It was turned down. He left town grumbling: "Every once in a while, you get taken by some riverboat gambler."

Good, gray John, a riverboat gambler?

Heavens, no.

Hell, yes.

Take your choice.

But the team belonged to Fetzer and his pals, and soon it was his alone, as he bought out all of his partners. He made another strong decision in 1962—one that would alter the direction of the Tigers. He named Jim Campbell as his general manager—and then made an even greater decision. He let Campbell run the show. Entirely. All Fetzer asked was a weekly report from Campbell and, please, run it like a business and keep the books in the black. He never asked for profits but did not want any losses, either. Campbell would say later, "Not once did Mr. Fetzer

S C R A P B O O K

"Baseball is essentially a business of muscles, with success riding on sharpness of reflexes and wholeheartedness of effort. Only occasionally, in this swing-from-heels era, does a ballplayer rise above the rest by using his head. One such man is George Kell, of the Detroit Tigers, who is generally regarded as the best third baseman in the game."

William Barry Furlong, *Saturday Evening Post*

◆

"During the game, the father of Tiger outfielder Rocky Colavito, sitting eight rows behind the Detroit dugout, got in a dispute with a fan who had been riding the Tigers. The rancorous argument attracted the attention of the players, and when Colavito saw that his father was involved he charged into the stands to help. It took four teammates, four policemen, three ushers, and an umpire to separate Rocky and his father's antagonist. Colavito and the fan were both ejected from the game.

"The next afternoon, as though in retaliation for his father's discomfort, Colavito unloaded on the Yankees, going four for five with two home runs and batting in half of Detroit's eight runs."

Ralph Houk with Robert W. Creamer, *Season of Glory*

◆

"Walter O. Briggs was, in the narrowest and best and most exacting sense of the term, a big leaguer. Among owners of baseball clubs, real big leaguers form a small and dwindling company, a company that has shrunk further with the death of the owner of the Detroit Tigers. Baseball cannot afford to lose his kind.

"Mr. Briggs was a sportsman, one of the very few in a game that has become, over the years, more and more a business and less and less a sport. He was not in baseball to make money, which he didn't need. He wasn't in it for personal publicity, which he didn't want.

"He did not look upon Briggs Stadium as a monument to himself. He considered it a place to play baseball, a place where fans like him could watch baseball, and because he was a fan and a big leaguer, he wanted it to be the best possible setting for the best possible baseball."

Red Smith, *New York Herald Tribune*, 1952

◆

"George is the quarterback of the team. George is all brains out there."

Harry Heilmann

◆

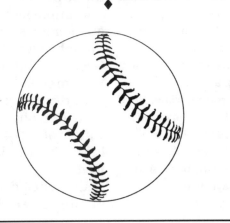

Bill Freehan learned some secrets of the catching craft from Hall of Famer Rick Ferrell, who starred in the majors from 1929 to 1947 before becoming a coach. ♦

Normally a second baseman, Billy Martin spent 1958 as a shortstop and third baseman with the Tigers, a clear indication of Detroit's decline. He came back to manage from 1971–1973, winning the 1972 American League East but losing the playoffs to Oakland. ♦

ever interfere with the operation of the ball club. He had his input but he let me make the decisions."

Campbell's own career with the Tigers had not had such an auspicious start. Shortly after joining the organization in 1949, Campbell was placed in charge of the farm team in Thomasville, Georgia. The ballpark burned down on him the first night.

Campbell lamented, "And I just had the ladies' room fixed up with drapes, paint, and a new linoleum floor."

In Detroit, the press box would burn down on him in the winter of 1974. This time Campbell said, "Can you imagine my luck? The whole thing burns down and there isn't a single writer in it."

Campbell dedicated his life to the ball club. He worked twelve months a year at his job. (Actually, he took Christmas Eve off.)

He was tough but fair with everyone. He lived through some trying experiences—from two of his managers dying on him in one year to one of his players—"Darling" Denny McLain—getting suspended three times in one season. Campbell, like many other G.M.s, hired and fired Billy Martin as manager. He went against his own principles by bringing Martin in but Bold Billy rewarded him by leading the Tigers to the Eastern Division title in 1972. They were beaten by Oakland in the playoffs and Martin was fired the following year with just 19 games left in the season.

At the start, Campbell could not judge talent. He admitted as much. He was primarily a businessman. So he did the next best thing—he surrounded himself with men who did know talent. Rick Ferrell, the old catcher, became Campbell's closest friend and chief adviser. Together, Campbell and Ferrell would build the Tigers into one of the most consistently successful teams in the major leagues.

DENNY AND
THE GANG

◆

L emme in! Come on, open the door! It's me, Norman! Open the door!"

It was eight o'clock in the morning, a Sunday morning in Kansas City. Jim Price was sound asleep in his room at the Muehlebach Hotel when he heard this pounding on the door. He knew immediately who it was. It was Stormin' Norman Cash, his roomie, back from a night on the town.

Price, the second string catcher on the Tigers, opened the door and Cash, the slugging first baseman, lurched into the room and fell on the bed.

"Uh, oh," Price thought. "I've got work to do."

The Tigers had a doubleheader scheduled that afternoon against Kansas City and Cash was expected to play in both games. Price looked down at him on the bed. Stormin' Norman was sound asleep.

Price went into the bathroom and turned on the shower. He picked up his roomie and carried him, fireman-style, over his shoulder into the bathroom. He stepped into the shower and held Cash under the running water.

Then the phone rang.

It was Cash's wife, calling from Detroit, wondering about where her husband was. Price handled the call and got her settled down. Cash, slowly awakening, started mumbling to himself. He was furious. He took his wristwatch off and threw it out of the open window.

"Norman, what are you doing!" Price cried out.

Cash fell over backwards into the bed, sound asleep again as soon as his body landed on the mattress.

Price went to the window and looked down. They were high

Norm Cash spent fifteen years as first sacker for Detroit after his initial two seasons with the White Sox. During seventeen campaigns, he slammed 377 homers and his .385 in the 1968 Series led the Tigers. ◆

Jim Price, a second-string catcher, stuck with the Tigers for five seasons. ♦

The 1968 team was among the most popular and exciting in Tiger history. "After twenty-three years without a pennant, and perhaps a decade without any good news of any description, Detroit could almost be forgiven for its susceptibility to the worst kind of baseball fever—the fence ripped down at the airport by the mob welcoming the team home; the billboards crying 'Tigertown, U.S.A.;' the tiger-striping on dresses, hats, suits, menus, and street crossings; the prefixative 'our' before every mention of the team in the papers; and the 'Sock It to 'Em, Tigers!' motto, with the excruciating variations ('Soc et Tuum, Tigres!' and 'Duro con Ellos, Tigres!') in every bar and department-store window."

Roger Angell, *The New Yorker* ♦

up in the hotel, but he could see the smashed watch in the middle of the street. Price took the elevator to the lobby and went out into the street after the watch. He knew it was expensive and thought maybe he could salvage enough of the pieces to have it repaired. As he bent over to pick up the small parts, he felt a tap on his shoulder.

"Can I help you?" asked a voice.

Price turned around and looked up. It was a policeman. "I think you'd better come with me," the cop said to Price.

Price looked down at himself. He had no shoes on and no pajama top. He'd come down into the empty street at eight o'clock in the morning in only his pajama bottoms, and he was being placed under arrest for indecent exposure.

At the police station, Price talked fast. He told them who he was and what had happened—discreetly leaving out some of the details about Stormin' Norman's condition. They bought his story and let him go without charges.

"Crazy? You bet it was crazy," Price would say in later years. "I mean, just picture this situation: Norman is out cold and I'm down at the police station in my pajama bottoms and we've got a doubleheader coming up and I don't know if either one of us can make it. It turned out that Bill Freehan was hurt and I had to catch both games that day. I go 0-for-8, but Cash bounces out of that bed with only a couple of hours of sleep and he gets six or seven hits in the doubleheader and we win both games. You talk about us having a wild, wild team in those days . . ."

The year was 1968. It was the Year of the Tiger in China. It was also the Year of the Tiger in baseball. The Tigers won it all—the pennant and the World Series—and maybe no team in history ever had a grander time reaching the top. They were a boisterous crew. They played hard on the field and they played hard off the field. They liked each other and hung out together and they had a manager who let them go—Mayo Smith, the old National Leaguer who was getting the ride of his life in Detroit and was smart enough not to put the brakes on.

The rules were simple: You met in the bar of the hotel after the game. You had a drink or two. Jim Price didn't drink, but he'd nurse a glass of tonic water and hoped nobody noticed. He didn't want to miss out on any of the fun.

When the gang had gathered, they'd go up to the suite they'd chipped in for and the party would begin. Food. Drinks. Cards. Girls. Talk. They even talked baseball at these parties. Sometimes the parties would last until the early hours of morning and only once did they make the mistake of getting a suite next to the one occupied by general manager Jim Campbell. He complained, mildly, about the noise. The players were also careful not to overdo the parties. They held them only on days which ended in "y."

The Tigers never lost a beat in the 1968 season. They got away fast and dominated the league, beating Baltimore by 12 games. Then they overcame the St. Louis Cardinals with a stirring comeback in the World Series, rallying from a three-games-to-one deficit and beating eventual Cy Young Award winner Bob Gibson in the final game in St. Louis. It was a season to end all

Manager Mayo Smith could afford to laugh as his club ran away with the pennant. He had known adversity running second division teams at Philadelphia and Cincinnati, and the Tiger victory was the only championship he ever achieved. ♦

seasons in Detroit, coming after the darkest year in the history of the city.

That was 1967. The Year of the Riot.

Few American cities have ever suffered the way Detroit did in that summer of '67. Watts had burned. Newark had burned, and now Detroit streets burned for almost five days and forty-three people were killed. Property damage was estimated in the millions. It was a time of terrible violence in America. Less than one year after the riot, Robert Kennedy and Martin Luther King would be victims of assassination, and violent campus unrest would rock the country.

In Detroit, it all started late on a Saturday night when a "blind pig," an after hours club, was raided by the cops on Twelfth Street in the heart of the black ghetto. By four o'clock Sunday afternoon, with the Yankees in town, billows of black smoke rose ominously over the rooftops back of left field. Nobody at the stadium grasped the scope of the situation. However, when the game ended, the Detroit players were instructed to return immediately to their homes—no dallying—and stay there. Most

Armed with rifles and bayonets, soldiers patrol a Detroit neighborhood in the aftermath of the 1967 civil disorders. ◆

lived in the suburbs, which were not threatened at the moment. But left fielder Willie Horton, who was raised on the streets of Detroit, still lived in downtown Detroit and he had to drive into the middle of the conflagration. He was appalled at what he saw. People were running wild through the smoke-filled streets, looting stores and carrying away radios, TV sets, clothes, liquor, anything they could lay their hands on.

The Tigers were scheduled to play in Detroit on Monday but the game was quickly switched to Baltimore. Horton, meanwhile, could not accept what he saw. He climbed into a truck and drove into the riot area—a black man talking to black people—and tried to settle them down. He told them he could understand their feelings but that they shouldn't be stealing other people's property. It was a courageous gesture on his part, but the violence went on unabated. What began as a confrontation with cops became open combat with troops of the National Guard.

And when the fires died out, it came down to the last day of the 1967 season. After second baseman Dick McAuliffe jammed into a season-ending double play, the hometown team was beaten out of the pennant on the final play of the final game. The frustration returned and so did the disorder.

The fans—mostly white—rioted in the ballpark. They stormed the field and battled with the stadium guards and city police. They even fought each other. They ripped up the pitcher's mound, tore out home plate, and flung chunks of grass into the air. Fights were breaking out everywhere among people who only moments earlier had been bonded together in their affection for a baseball team. Now they were flailing out at everyone around them, throwing chairs on the field and tossing cushions into the dugouts in frustration and rage. The final standings:

Willie Horton, with 36 homers, helped propel the 1968 team into the World Series where he hit .304. In the days following the civil disorders of 1967 Horton sought on his own to calm citizens. ◆

	W	L	Pct.	GE
Boston	92	70	.568	—
Detroit	91	71	.562	1
Minnesota	91	71	.562	1

It was the lowest point in the history of baseball in Detroit.

Fear gripped the city in the spring of 1968. Everyone wondered what would happen when the streets started heating up again. More people bought more guns in Detroit in 1968 than at anytime in the city's history till then. The city literally became an armed camp in the spring of '68. Everyone expected the worst.

But a strange thing started happening at the corner of Michigan and Trumbull. The ball club began winning games. They

Mickey Lolich not only won three games in the 1968 World Series but he also hit his first major league homer in Game 2. ♦

Dick McAuliffe survived at the plate with one of the most awkward-appearing stances in the league. He served as shortstop or second sacker for fourteen seasons. In *I Don't Care If I Never Come Back,* Art Hill called him "the most determined hitter I ever saw." ♦

Resourceful Tigers fans crane to catch a view of a 1968 World Series game. ♦

won them in exciting fashion, coming from behind in the seventh, eighth, and ninth innings. Each game seemed to produce new drama. The players took turns at providing the heroics.

Here was Willie Horton, a black man, waiting at the plate to shake the hand of Norm Cash, a white man; and here was the catcher, Bill Freehan, a white man, going to the mound to offer words of encouragement to pitcher Earl Wilson, a black man. It was like the middle 1930s all over again; a city caught in a great social struggle could suddenly find a diversion for itself. It found a reason to feel good again—a reason to feel some pride again.

Suddenly, there was a sense of joy in the city. People started listening to the games on the radio and following them on TV. You could walk through entire alleys and not miss one of broadcaster Ernie Harwell's calls blaring through the open windows. Suddenly, there was a place to go—Michigan and Trumbull—where you could have a little fun for yourself.

Jim Northrup's triple knocked in a pair in Game 7 to put his team ahead for good. ♦

The players themselves were confident in that spring of 1968. They felt they had the best team and should have won the pennant in 1967. Now they were determined to make up for it. They started the season with confidence, and their confidence grew to tremendous proportions with each success, until they became an irresistible, rip-roaring team that could not be stopped by anyone. A man who drank twenty-five Pepsi-Colas a day led the way.

If the 1968 season belonged to anyone, it belonged to Dennis Dale McLain. He was The Imp. The one who threw his high, hard fast one past everyone and laughed at the world around him. Nothing was impossible for Dennis Dale McLain in 1968. The world—which included stage, screen, and radio—was his for the taking. That's what happens when you win 31 games. Nobody asks questions. Everything you do is "cute"—even stiffing people for money, which is what Dennis Dale did throughout his days in Detroit. He borrowed money he didn't return, flew in airplanes he didn't own, using gas he didn't pay for. Who cared? Just keep throwing that high, hard one, Denny. We all love you.

It was a truly incredible season for this man. Dennis Dale became the first pitcher to win 30 games since Dizzy Dean in 1934.

Yet remarkable as his season was, McLain was not the only hero that year. The Tigers had enough heroes for everyone. Gates Brown hit .370 as a pinch hitter. Jim Northrup banged four grand-slam homers in regulation and another in the World Series. A young pitcher by the name of Darryl Patterson stunned a national television audience by coming into a game with the bases loaded in Baltimore and striking out the side. A freckle-

Denny McLain kicks high before firing to the plate in September 1968 as he drives toward his 31 wins and a Detroit pennant. ◆

Gates Brown pinch-hit himself into Detroit history with two league-leading seasons in that category. In 1968 he hit safely in 18 of his 39 attempts for an astonishing .461 average. ◆

Mickey Stanley brought a marvelous glove to center field. It was Mayo Smith's brilliant idea to insert him at shortstop for the 1968 World Series, where he committed only two errors of no importance. Stanley lasted for fifteen seasons in spite of a mediocre bat. ◆

faced kid named Tom Matchick, who looked like he could have been the bat boy, stunned the Orioles again with a pinch-hit home run with two on in the ninth inning.

It was not all sweetness and light. Second baseman Dick McAuliffe fought with Chicago pitcher Tommy John, drawing a five-day suspension. The players wound up in a beanball contest in Oakland with one of them throwing a ball into the stands and hitting a woman spectator. She sued for $200,000 and collected an unspecified amount of cash. Pitcher Joe Sparma claimed manager Mayo Smith didn't treat him like a man and blasted Smith in the newspapers, just two days after the newspapers came back from a season-long strike. Willie Horton was knocked unconscious in a collision with shortstop Ray Oyler, who was 45 pounds lighter than Horton. Al Kaline suffered a fractured arm and missed six weeks of the season. Pitcher Earl Wilson was conked by two line drives in the same inning. The first was a triple-carom shot off his shoulder, jaw, and thumb. The second ripped into his pitching hand. Wilson nearly had two fights with McLain, once over McLain eating his peaches from the refrigerator in the clubhouse. McLain left him a note: "The Phantom Strikes Again!" Third baseman Don Wert was beaned. Veteran Eddie Mathews suffered a herniated disc in his back and was out for most of the season. McAuliffe got so angry at striking out one day that he slammed his bat to the ground and it bounced back against his thigh and knocked him out of commission.

However, when October rolled around, they were healthy enough to win one of the most memorable World Series in recent history.

Denny McLain, with his 31 wins and his flapping tongue, naturally had the spotlight for the 1968 World Series. In Game 1, however, he was up against one of baseball's gutsiest pitchers, Bob Gibson, whose 22–9 record included an e.r.a. of 1.12. Gibson fanned a World Series–record seventeen Tigers. McLain hit the showers in the sixth inning. Final score: 4–0, Cardinals.

In the second inning of Game 2, Willie Horton broke the Tiger drought with a blast into the left field seats. In the third inning, pitcher Mickey Lolich, a man with five motorcycles in the basement of his home, reached the seats for the only homer in his career. Norm Cash chipped in another four-bagger and it was an 8–1 laugher for Lolich.

The Cardinals showed the long ball themselves in Game 3 with three-run shots by Tim McCarver and Orlando Cepeda, which far outstripped Al Kaline's two-run homer and the solo shot from Dick McAuliffe. Bob Gibson returned in Game 4 to limit the

The Tigers obtained Earl Wilson from the Boston Red Sox during the 1966 season. In 1967, his first full year with the club, the big righty topped his league, winning 22 while losing only 11. ◆

132

TIGERS

The smoke of fireworks shrouds Tiger Stadium as the team celebrates capturing the pennant with a 2–1 win over the Yankees. Second place Baltimore finished 12 games back as Detroit clinched on September 17. ♦

Tigers to a single run—a homer from Bill Northrup—as the Cardinals won 10–1. McLain lasted only into the third inning. Now the Cardinals led three games to one.

Detroit staved off defeat in Game 5 only after Lou Brock, who stole seven bases in the Series, for some inexplicable reason failed to slide at the plate in the fifth inning. On second with a double, Brock raced for home on a Julian Javier single to left. Catcher Bill Freehan held the ball from Willie Horton's throw as Brock crashed into him. *Out!* signaled umpire Doug Harvey. Brock disputed the call vigorously, but replay film showed that Harvey had called it right. Then, in the seventh inning, instead of yanking the weak-hitting Lolich for a pinch-hitter (in the season, Lolich hit .114) Manager Mayo Smith decided he preferred Lolich's arm in the game. Lolich surprised everyone with a soft single that loaded the bases. Al Kaline's single then put Detroit ahead and the final score was 5–3. Lolich won his second.

In Game 6, the Tigers went beserk in the third inning, pushing across ten runs, highlighted by Northrup's grand slam. It was a 13–1 win for McLain.

But Game 7 put the dreaded Gibson back on the mound for

Al Kaline races to the deepest area of Yankee Stadium to glove a long drive. ◆

Catcher Bill Freehan blocks the plate and tags Lou Brock out after the Cardinal outfielder tried to score on a single to Willie Horton in left. The Cardinals led 3–2 at the time and some believe Brock would have been safe had he slid. The Tigers eventually won the game. ◆

"All my life somebody has been a big star and Lolich was No. 2. I figured my day would come and this was it."
—Mickey Lolich, after winning seventh game of 1968 World Series. ◆

Norm Cash led both leagues with .361 in 1961 and finished second in total bases only to Roger Maris, who broke Ruth's record with 61 homers. ◆

the Cardinals. Although Lolich had had only two days off, he was the best available arm. The visiting Tigers failed to score in the first six innings. In the home half of the sixth Brock singled to start the assault. He took a 20-foot lead. In a similar situation in Game 2, when Lolich had thrown to first, Brock had sprinted to second and beaten the peg from Norm Cash. But Lolich could not afford to allow such a lead in a scoreless game, and he whipped the ball to first. Brock took off for second. The throw from Cash zipped past Brock where shortstop Mickey Stanley took it and slapped the ball on Brock for an out. With two outs, Curt Flood reached first on a single. Again he led off and *déjà vu*, Lolich picked him off, just as he had Brock.

In the seventh inning, the Tigers put a pair on with two out. Jim Northrup lined to center, where Flood seemed to slip momentarily and the ball rolled to the wall for a triple. Eventually, three runs came home that inning and with one more in the ninth, Detroit won 4–1, taking the World Series.

Although the Tigers had many heroes that season, no one—mortal or otherwise—made a greater impact on the game of baseball, not to mention the game of life, than Dennis Dale McLain in that summer of '68.

He came to the Tigers as a brash young pitcher in 1963. He was the son-in-law of Hall of Famer Lou Boudreau and acted like a Hall of Famer himself from the very outset. There was nothing he couldn't do. (Just ask him.) There was nothing he was afraid to say. He was the best interview in the clubhouse, and it didn't seem to matter that he could never keep his facts straight. He was colorful and that was enough for everyone. Anyone who could drink twenty-five Pepsi's a day, play the organ in his spare time, and win 31 games in a season was, quite clearly, a very special person who deserved special privileges.

Denny had let the team down badly in 1967, but this was quickly overlooked as his victories mounted up in 1968.

One day, in the final weeks of the '67 season, Denny limped into the clubhouse. He couldn't pitch. At first he said he didn't know how he hurt his foot. He said it fell asleep on him and he twisted it when he stepped on it. Then he claimed it happened as he was getting out of bed. Then he said it happened in the garage. Nobody could follow these stories, much less understand them, since they seemed to change from day to day. Another account held that the Mafia had smashed his foot because he was reneging on a debt. This supposedly occurred in a pool hall. Then the damage was allegedly done on a private boat. The facts were never revealed, and Denny stopped talking about it after a while. He wasn't pitching much, either, and when he did—as

Dick McAuliffe steadied the infield at second, particularly when outfielder Mickey Stanley was brought in during the World Series to handle shortstop. Here he turns a double play against the Cardinals while the prone Orlando Cepeda can only watch. Bill Freehan (below) bears the burden of Mickey Lolich after the final out of Game 7 in which Lolich limited St. Louis to a single run while his colleagues racked up four. ◆

John Hiller, blasted in his Series relief appearances, could afford to horse around with Cash after the seventh game win. ◆

in the final game of the season—he was ineffective. A lot of people blamed him for losing the pennant.

Yet, when McLain got it rolling in '68, his transgressions were quickly forgotten. He became the darling of the city . . . even to those people he was conning out of money.

On April 11, the second day of the season, McLain got his first start. He was pressed into duty when Mickey Lolich was summoned to National Guard duty following the assassination of Martin Luther King, Jr. McLain was not involved in the decision but the brownish-blond-haired pitcher showed the fans something new: a mop of red hair.

Principals in the success of the 1968 club, Norm Cash, Al Kaline, and Bill Freehan (standing left to right), Dick McAuliffe, and Denny McLain seated, made the American League All-Star team in 1966. ◆

McLain was more than a flash of brilliance; from 1965–1969 he recorded 108 victories. When the troubles began in 1970, he was still only 26. ◆

The Tigers were on their way to a nine-game winning streak which would put them in first place for the rest of the season.

McLain won his first game ten days later, missing a shutout against Chicago on Pete Ward's home run in the ninth inning. This was one of the last quiet moments of the year for Dennis Dale.

On May 1, McLain beat Minnesota, but he was raging all over the place after the game. Three times he struck out Tony Oliva, the Twins' star slugger, and told everyone that if he kept pitching like that, he would want one million dollars in 1969. The Twins hit two home runs off him and Denny said the Detroit ballpark was so small that "the owners could take it and throw it in the Atlantic Ocean." Everyone wrote down every word. Denny also denied he had dyed his hair.

On May 5, McLain ran his record to 4—0 and sounded off about the Detroit fans. With the reporters jammed around his locker—they knew where the good quotes were—Denny called the Detroit fans "the biggest front-runners in the world." He said, "Norm Cash and I were going bad last season and they got all over us. How do you think a guy's wife feels when her husband is going 0-for-8 or 0-for-16 and the fans are booing him while she's up in the stands? If they think we're stupid for playing this game, how stupid are they for watching us?"

McLain looks the personification of the family man in this photo from the summer of 1968, but he could not resist the temptations that came with his fame, and his career sank in the mud of vice. ◆

The reporters raced back to the press box to write these luscious comments. After they were gone, Denny started thinking about what he had said. Tom Loomis of the *Toledo Blade* was still around. Denny called Loomis over to his locker and told him, "When I said those things, I only meant one percent of the fans."

Too late.

Detroit management was outraged when it read Denny's comments in the papers the next day. When the Tigers went to Baltimore, management arranged an appearance for McLain on Ernie Harwell's pre-game show. Denny explained the part about one percent of the fans. The ploy didn't work. The fans jumped all over him during his next appearance at Tiger Stadium.

The unhappiness didn't last long, however. McLain started winning games every fourth day—one performance more impressive than the other. On May 25, he beat the Oakland A's 2–1 and worked out of a ninth inning jam by fanning Reggie Jackson. The fans ate it up. On June 13, he ran his record to 10–2 and his crop of brownish-blond hair was back. He said: "I did not dye my hair, no matter what anyone says. It was Mother Nature."

McLain added a note of mystery to his saga. He revealed that a smoke bomb had been found under the hood of his wife's car. He said a gas station attendant discovered it while checking the oil. Denny remarked that the bomb had been wired incorrectly.

Denny ran his record to 12–2 in Boston on June 20. He had a no-hitter going until the seventh, when George Scott singled to left with two out and the ball grazed the glove of shortstop Ray Oyler. When asked what he said when he saw the ball roll into short left field, McLain replied, "I said, 'Fudge.'"

He won his fifteenth game on July 5. Afterwards, he told the mob of reporters, "I don't consider myself the best pitcher in the league. I consider myself the best pitcher only on the nights I go out to pitch."

He won his sixteenth game on July 7, beating Oakland in the first game of a doubleheader in Detroit. He climbed to the organ loft during the second game and serenaded the fans with his rendition of "Satin Doll." As he left the organ loft, he said, "What's the matter with the amplifier? I'll send up a man to check it."

McLain was picked for the All-Star game in Houston. He flew to Las Vegas in a borrowed plane the day before the game, then flew to Houston, worked two scoreless innings, and flew back to Las Vegas. "I like Las Vegas," he said.

Mayo Smith managed to keep Denny McLain from self-destructing for several turbulent years but 1970 was Mayo's last season and Denny's first big suspension. ◆

On July 27, McLain won his twentieth game—the first pitcher since Lefty Grove in 1931 to reach 20 victories by the month of July. The Tigers were 7-½ games ahead and Denny credited the newspaper strike for the bulge. "The big thing is that the writers are not around demoralizing the players."

He won No. 21 on July 31, shutting out Washington 4–0. He said it was his first shutout in Tiger Stadium in a long time. "I hate this park," he said. "I hate it, I hate it, I hate it." That afternoon, a new organ was delivered to his home: an X-77, courtesy of the Hammond Organ Co. He said, "I'm going with Hammond this year." He said he would introduce the organ at a recital in New York, and also show it in Las Vegas—". . . at the Riviera, get it right"—when the season was over.

A writer asked Denny if he was getting money hungry.

"No, I'm not money hungry," he replied. "Yes, I'm money hungry."

Denny ran his record to 23–3 with a 13–1 victory over Cleveland. With the Detroit newspapers back in business, he told the writers that he had cut five sides of an album the afternoon of the game. He said, "We cut one eighteen times and finally got it and then missed the last chord and threw the whole thing out." Scribble, scribble, scribble.

When he won No. 24, Denny said he expected to be paid $200,000 in 1969. He also said that *Time* and *Life* were after him for stories and that he would be appearing on the Ed Sullivan and Joey Bishop shows on television. Scribble, scribble, scribble.

"The recital in New York will be at the Hampshire House, if any of you stiffs are interested," he said. He added, "Yes, I'm thinking about winning 30 games."

When he was in New York, Denny was interviewed by *Time*, *Life*, and UPI. He told Milton Richman of UPI that it was remarkable that he was pitching at all since he had a torn muscle in his shoulder. Richman put the story out on his national wire and it created headlines from coast to coast. When Denny got back to Detroit, the reporters asked him about his torn shoulder muscle. They wondered how he could win so many games and throw so hard with a torn muscle. He said, "It's nothing real, real serious. It's only torn to the extent that it's stretched."

On September 1, with the Orioles making a last-ditch attempt to catch the Tigers, McLain beat them in Tiger Statium and started a triple play in the bargain. He snared a liner off the bat of John Powell and threw it to shortstop Tom Matchick, doubling off Curt Blefary. Matchick relayed the ball to first base to get Brooks Robinson. It was a spectacular play.

On the plane ride to Anaheim that night, McLain was standing in the galley with several of his teammates and a reporter. He said he had never been so scared in his life.

"What do you mean?" asked the reporter.

"Powell's ball, didn't you see it? It was headed straight for my face," Denny said. "If I don't get my glove up there, it smashes into the eyeglasses and maybe I'm blind forever."

The next day, the Detroit newspapers showed McLain catching Powell's drive at his belt buckle.

When the Tigers were in Anaheim, Denny spent a day conferring with the Smothers Brothers over a possible TV appearance. He was impressed by their home. "What a pad they've got," he said. "It cost something like four hundred thousand dollars. I want one like it someday."

Denny won No. 29 on September 10, and Ed Sullivan went into the Detroit clubhouse looking for him. Denny introduced him to all the other players. Denny left the ballpark with singer Glen Campbell, telling him, "I always wanted to be in show business."

Finally, the big day arrived: September 14, 1968: The day Dennis Dale McLain was to try for 30. Oakland was in town and Denny told everyone he didn't like the pictures of himself in *Life* magazine, especially the ones that showed him sitting in the dugout, yawning.

Dizzy Dean, the last 30-game winner, showed up for the momentous occasion. Watson Spoelstra, chairman of the Detroit Baseball Writer's Association, threw Dean out of the press box, grumbling that he was not a writer. Denny won a close one in the ninth and twenty years later, while appearing on Bob Costas's coast-to-coast radio show, Denny revealed that when Willie Horton got the winning hit to left with two out in the ninth, he jumped off the bench, hit his head on the dugout, and knocked himself out for a moment. He told Costas, "Pay no attention to that cover on *Sports Illustrated* showing me and Al Kaline racing up the steps of the dugout. Al was holding me up, trying to steady me. I was out."

They were tremendous times for the Tigers, climaxed by their seventh-game Series victory over the Cardinals in St. Louis. The Tigers set off a city-wide celebration that lasted all night long, people hugging and kissing, drinking, dancing, and laughing until the light of dawn streaked the skies . . . just one year after the city had set fire to itself. Sadly, six men on the 1968 championship team have died—manager Mayo Smith, pitchers Joe Sparma and Don McMahon, first baseman Norm Cash, shortstop Ray Oyler, and infielder-outfielder Bob Christian.

McLain's disappointing turn in the '68 Series (1–2 record) included a home run ball to Lou Brock in Game Four. ◆

Premier Denny McLain follows through on his way to 31 wins, 6 losses for an amazing .838 percentage in 1968. He struck out 280 in 336 innings. ◆

McLain met his demise in quite a different manner, first getting suspended three times in one season and, later, in private life, spending twenty-nine months in a Federal penitentiary on charges of conspiracy, loansharking, and drug trafficking. He also declared bankruptcy twice, and his home in Tampa burned, destroying his two Cy Young plaques and his Most Valuable Player award.

As McLain could do no wrong in 1968, he could do no right in 1970. No player in history ever squandered more wealth and talent in a shorter period of time than this man. Commissioner Bowie Kuhn suspended him until July 1 of 1970 for his involvement in a bookmaking establishment in Flint, Michigan.

Poor Denny. He paid the bills and his partners took the profits. His downfall started when a story in *Sports Illustrated* revealed his connections with the mob.

Eventually, McLain's tangled finances became public knowledge. Though he had been earning an estimated $200,000 a year, his lawyers filed a bankruptcy petition on his behalf that listed a debt of $446,069. His assets were listed as $413. He

S C R A P B O O K

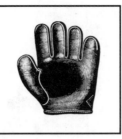

"This is a 24-year-old boy reaching for Utopia. You accept what he is and work with that. But this is what makes him a great pitcher. He's brash enough. You can't take that brashness away from him, and you wouldn't want to. I like him for what he is."

Mayo Smith on Denny McLain in 1968

◆

"Surprisingly, the Tigers themselves, gathered around the cage during batting practice, seemed in remarkable fettle for a group apparently awaiting only the executioner's blindfold. Norm Cash was telling George Kell . . . that he had just figured out how to hit Gibson. 'It's like duck-shooting,' he said. 'You gotta *lead* the goddam bird. When he's up here [he imitated Gibson at the top of his windup], you gotta start swinging. Pow!' "

Roger Angell, *The New Yorker*, 1968

◆

"I thought to myself, 'There is Al Kaline, sixteen years in the big leagues, never played in a World Series.' I knew it was the perfect sport for him. I wanted him to get a base hit, for my sake naturally, and for the team's sake. But not so much for myself and for the team, but for himself. If anybody could get that hit, I wanted it to be Al Kaline."

Mickey Lolich after Kaline drove home two runners in the seventh inning of World Series Game 5, bringing the Tigers from behind to a 4–3 lead.

◆

"I had to like Mayo's beautiful answer to a reporter who wanted to know how it felt to be looking ahead to a single game for the World's Championship in which the Tigers would have to face that nearly perfect pitching man, Bob Gibson.

" 'Why,' the good-natured balding man said in typical slow talking fashion, 'I must say I feel a helluva lot better about going against Gibson tomorrow . . . than I would about going home tonight.' "

Si Burick, The *Dayton Daily News*

◆

"So the Series came down to its last game and the confrontation, it turned out, was between Gibson and Lolich. Both had won two games, and both had tired arms, though Lolich was starting with one less day of rest. He pitched the first two innings like a man defusing a live bomb, working slowly and unhappily, and studying the problem at length before the new move. He threw mostly sidearm, aiming at corners and often missing. After he had defused Brock for the second time, in the third, he seemed to gain poise and began getting ahead of the hitters."

Roger Angell, *The New Yorker*

◆

As a teenager with the Tigers, McLain hurt himself with walks. Unfortunately, as he grew older and gained control of his pitching game, he lost control of his personal life and career. ◆

owed eighty-three creditors. The Tigers were listed as one of those creditors, having advanced Denny $39,386 on his 1970 salary. On one occasion, Denny went to a Detroit bank in an attempt to negotiate a $25,000 loan. The bank called the Tigers and asked if his contract would cover that amount. The Tigers told them it wouldn't. The bank granted the loan anyway.

The IRS moved in and claimed McLain's furniture to satisfy a tax bill of $9,460. The seizure included his Hammond organ.

McLain returned to the game on July 1, 1970, and a sellout crowd of 53,863—largest in eight years—turned out for the occasion. While Denny was now a curiosity piece to many fans, others still adored him. They could not forget those 31 victories and said they didn't care about what he did in his private life, as long as he could still throw that high, hard one.

McLain lasted 5-⅓ innings against the Yankees and was not involved in the decision. Denny was back, but not for long. On August 28, he threw buckets of water over the heads of two sportswriters, and General Manager Jim Campbell of the Tigers suspended him. Campbell said the suspension would be for a period of not more than thirty days. Each day Denny was losing $500 in salary.

As it turned out, the suspension was to last only seven days. Campbell planned to lift it on September 5. On September 4, Commissioner Kuhn reentered the picture. He ordered the Tigers to bring McLain to his New York office, where Kuhn placed him under suspension again for violating his probation by carrying a gun on a Tiger trip.

On at least one occasion, in a restaurant in Chicago, McLain had flashed the gun to his teammates.

His days with Detroit came to an end in Cincinnati on the eve of the 1970 World Series between Cincinnati and Baltimore. The Tigers upstaged the World Series by calling a press conference and announcing they had traded their troubled pitcher to the Washington Senators. McLain said he felt fine, physically. He said he had a certificate from his doctor stating that he was sane. He wondered if the writers had similar documents in their possession.

On the way back to the hotel after the press conference, Campbell tossed something into the gutter and murmured to himself: "I won't be needing these anymore."

It was a roll of Tums.

THE BIRD AND OTHER FLIGHTS OF FANCY

♦

The date was July 3, 1906. Don't bother looking it up in any of the baseball history books. Nothing much happened on that day except that Germany Schaefer of the Tigers decided to play one inning against the Cleveland Indians while wearing a raincoat.

Interesting guy, Germany. He played second base for the Tigers and one day in Chicago, he was sent up as a pinch-hitter against the White Sox. The umpire turned and yelled to the fans, "Schaefer batting next!" They did not have public address systems in those days and the umpires had to announce the changes. Schaefer waddled toward the plate and he, too, turned to face the stands. The ump's introduction hadn't suited him. It was too abrupt. Too impersonal. No pizzazz. Germany shouted out: "Ladies and gentlemen, we present Herman Schaefer, the world's champion batsman, who will now give a demonstration of his great batting skill."

The fans began to jeer. They were laughing. Some of them threw their scorecards on the field.

Schaefer stepped into the batter's box and got set. He proceeded to knock the ball over the left field fence.

He took off for first base, sliding into the base and shouting: "The Prince leads at the quarter!" He slid into second base and cried out: "It's the Prince at the halfway pole!" He hit the dirt at third and called out: "It's the Prince by a mile!" He finally slid into home plate, rose, dusted off his uniform, and doffed his cap to the fans. "That, ladies and gentlemen, concludes The Great Prince Schaefer's afternoon performance." He bowed and walked back to the dugout.

Which brings us to Bill Faul, a Detroit pitcher in the early

Herman "Germany" Schaefer spent four colorful years in Detroit, 1905–1909. A .257 lifetime hitter, he smote only 9 homers in fifteen seasons. ♦

1960s. He was an interesting one, too. He was a sidearm pitcher who would talk to himself on the mound while cocking his head to one side to get a better angle on the plate. When he was asked for the secret of his success, limited as it was, he said: "Hypnotism."

Hypnotism?

"Yes, hypnotism," he said. "I put myself under before going out to pitch."

None of the writers believed him, but they all wrote about it. After all, a story was a story, and things could get pretty dull in the middle of training camp.

Faul said he would look into the mirror and hypnotize himself. He said it was very relaxing. He said if someone knocked one into the upper deck, it didn't bother him. Everyone went along with the gag, including a girl who lived in Lakeland, Florida, the training base of the Tigers. Faul told her of his hypnotic powers and asked if she'd like a demonstration. "Well, yes," she said hesitantly. Faul went outside and pulled one wheel of his car up on the curb. He told the girl to sit in the doorway and stare at

In addition to intimate chats with the ball, and exuberant encouragement of his mates, Fidrych was an exacting groundskeeper every inning. ◆

the car. He turned on one of the signal lights and, as it was blinking in her eyes, he said: "Sleeeeeeeep . . . Sleeeeeeeep . . . "

On the other hand, Cletis "Boots" Poffenberger was a pitcher in the late 1930s who was blinded by the bright lights of major league baseball. He loved to live it up. In fact, some days he did not show up for work. He became known as the "Duke of Duck-out." Poffenberger never tried to hide his penchant for fun, and after a night on the town, he would call room service from his hotel room and ask if they would send up "The Breakfast of Champions."

"And what is that, sir?"

"Two fried eggs and a beer," he would answer.

Charlie Maxwell, the popular outfielder in the middle 1950s, liked to have fun with the reporters. He was known as Paw Paw after his home town of Paw Paw, Michigan.

Maxwell: "I used to be a newspaperman."

Reporter: "Really?"

Maxwell: "Yeah, I used to work for a tri-weekly."

Reporter: "A tri-weekly?"

Maxwell: "We tried to put it out weekly."

One day, Maxwell went into the coffee shop of the Hotel Shoreham in Washington where a newspaperman was drinking a milk shake before heading out to the ballpark.

"Whatcha drinking there?" Maxwell asked.

"A coffee milk shake," said the writer.

"A coffee milk shake!" exclaimed Maxwell. "You gotta be kidding."

"Nope," said the writer. "I have to have something to keep me awake when I watch you guys play."

Cletis "Boots" Poffenberger aroused great expectations with a 10–5 season as a rookie in 1937. But his performance never approached the heights of his antics and the Tigers waived him in 1939. He was picked up by the Brooklyn Dodgers for whom he yielded 7 hits in a total of five innings before disappearing from major league ball forever. ◆

A frustrated Bob Swift gloves another high soft one behind the plate for the Tigers as 3'7" Eddie Gaedel pinch-hits for the St. Louis Browns. ◆

"Maybe so," replied Maxwell, "but I'll bet more people have gone to sleep reading newspapers than watching ball games."

Gates Brown and Willie Horton were close friends on the Tigers in the 1960s and '70s. But they were not beyond kidding each other. One night they spoke at a school banquet in Detroit. A young boy asked a question: "Mr. Brown, what did you take when you were in high school?"

Horton stood up. "I'll answer that," he said. "When Gates was in high school, he took arithmetic, spelling, geography, and overcoats."

Bob Swift, who managed the Tigers briefly in 1965, told the players what he expected of them in the matter of personal conduct when the team was on the road. "We go first class," Swift said. "When we check out of the hotels, we don't take the towels. We take the TV sets."

Swift, who had a good sense of humor, had been the catcher on that memorable day—August 19, 1951—when owner Bill Veeck of the St. Louis Browns sent a midget to the plate against the Tigers.

That was Eddie Gaedel, No. $\frac{1}{8}$ on your scorecard. He was $3\frac{1}{2}$ feet tall, weighed 50 pounds, and came out of the St. Louis dugout swinging half a dozen drugstore bats.

This was Veeck's idea of fun. He had promised his fans a few surprises if they came out for the doubleheader against the Tigers. He gave them some jugglers, jitterbug dancers, and a ragtime band between the games. But he saved the best for last. When the Browns came to the plate in the bottom of the first inning of the second game, right fielder Frank Saucier was supposed to lead off. But a midget came walking to the plate.

"What's going on?" said Swift, suppressing a grin.

"Yeah," demanded umpire Ed Hurley. "What's going on?" He was not smiling.

Manager Zack Wheat of the Browns walked to the plate. He held an American League contract with Eddie Gaedel's name on it. Hurley looked at the document, then stared at Wheat. He knew he was being duped, but couldn't do anything about it.

"Okay, play ball," said Hurley, exceedingly irritated.

Bob Cain, the Detroit pitcher, peered in at Swift for the sign. Swift didn't give him a sign.

"Just keep it low," called Swift.

Swift got down on his knees and held his glove up as a target for Cain. No good. Cain walked the midget on four pitches while the crowd went wild. Veeck, up in the press box, was beside himself with glee.

"I thought maybe we should hit him," said Swift. "But I didn't want to face a homicide charge."

Bill Armour, who managed the Tigers in 1905 and '06, was another character. He tried to show people that he was in command by wearing street clothes on the bench. No mere uniform for him. Armour didn't fool anyone, because they all knew that before he made any decisions, he would stop by the private box where his wife sat and ask for her advice. Not only was he a jittery man, but Armour was also very superstitious. Whenever he saw a butterfly on the field, he made the umpire halt the game and had his players kill it.

Dave Rozema, who pitched for the Tigers in the 1980s, was considered one of the team's all-time flakes. He was always pulling pranks on his teammates, but he was very serious one day outside of his motel in Lakeland. That's the day he decided to wash his new car and used Brillo soap pads to get it really clean.

Paul Foytack, a Tigers pitcher in the 1950s, was a man with a keen sense of humor. One year the Tigers decided to screen in the lower deck in right field to make it harder to hit home runs. When a newspaperman asked Foytack for his reaction, he said, "That's great—now what about the upper deck?"

The Tigers had some genuine characters in the 1950s. Pitcher Frank Lary decided one night he would dump a pail of fish in the swimming pool of the Holiday Inn in Lakeland. Nobody no-

Frank Lary, known as "Taters" to his teammates, posted better than 20 wins in 1956 and 1961. Because he was so effective against the New Yorkers, once even beating them with a squeeze bunt himself, they also called him "The Yankee Killer." ♦

ticed until Billy Hoeft, another pitcher, decided to wade in after them.

Bored with life in spring training, Lary decided to travel across the county line for a few drinks. But he had no transportation, so he "borrowed" the team bus.

Johnny Groth, an outfielder in the 1940s and 1950s, abhorred any kind of bugs, so naturally his teammates filled his locker, his pants pockets, and his shoes with crickets, beetles, spiders, and ants.

Groth lived in Chicago and had five daughters. But when the Tigers would play in Chicago, he wouldn't go home. He'd stay at the team's hotel. "Gotta get my rest," he would say.

Rusty Staub was a fusspot in his days in Detroit in the late 1970s. He insisted on a contract stipulating that airport runways had to be a certain length before he would get on any plane with the Tigers. He also took naps in the clubhouse before games, and wore two sets of gloves during the games—one for batting and one for base running.

Willie Horton hated to fly, so his teammates would lock him in the men's room at the back of the plane. Horton was afraid of a lot of things, especially dead animals. You can imagine his reaction the day in Boston when he hit a foul ball straight up into the air and—plop!—a dead pigeon fell from the sky and landed smack on home plate. Horton backed away from the plate so fast, he almost toppled into the stands.

Ray Boone, a third baseman in the late '50s, was another bad flyer with the Tigers. One time the team was flying from Detroit to Kansas City for a weekend series when one of the plane's four engines conked out. The aircraft had to be diverted to Chicago. The Tigers got another plane and continued to Kansas City.

The following Sunday night, the players were getting on a plane to fly back to Detroit. Boone paused. He pulled a small piece of paper out of his pocket, on which he had written some numbers. They were the numbers of the plane that had been forced to land in Chicago. The numbers matched. This was the same plane. "See you later, guys," said Boone. He took the train back to Detroit.

Coach George Myatt was another who hated flying. His tactic was very simple. He downed as many double martinis as he could swallow while the team waited at the airport to board the plane.

The Tigers' first flight ever was in the spring of 1957. The players had talked owner Spike Briggs into allowing them to fly from Lakeland to Houston, where they would play a weekend exhibition series. Briggs was apprehensive about allowing his team to go up in the air. He finally agreed only if the pilot didn't

go out over the Gulf of Mexico but followed the coastline of Florida around to Texas. What did the Tigers know about flying in those days? They had a small two-engine DC-3 and packed everything on board—luggage, trunks, bats, balls, gloves, uniforms . . . and the three extra players that they were permitted to use at the start of spring training. They took off from Drain Field in Lakeland. The plane was so heavy it ran off the end of the runway and bounced through a field, struggling to get airborne. A reporter looked out the window and saw the grass under the plane. His face went white. Trainer Jack Homel was sitting across the way and started laughing. "Your biggest story," he said, "and you won't be able to write it." At that moment, the plane slowly lifted from the ground, but Homel kept on laughing. A few years later, the laugh was on him.

The Tigers were in New York and Homel was in his hotel room sleeping. The phone rang. It was Frank Contway, the club's traveling secretary. He was calling from the lobby and he wanted Homel to come down and have a drink with him.

"You're crazy . . . it's the middle of the night," said Homel, and hung up.

Pretty soon there was a knock on the door. It was Contway. Still feeling a little high, he wouldn't take no for an answer.

"Go away, I'm sleeping," growled Homel, who was stark naked as he peeked around the partially opened door.

John T. Groth (left) was a consistent contact hitter. During a fifteen-year career, he compiled a lifetime average of .279, with a high of .306 in 1950.

Burly Steve Bilko (right) smacked 56 homers in one minor league season but never showed power in the majors. He was a member of the raggedy Tigers of 1960, the club that ran through three managers: Jimmy Dykes, Billy Hitchcock, and Joe Gordon, who quit immediately after the season. ♦

Contway saw his condition, reached in and grabbed Homel by the wrist, and pulled him into the hallway.

Click!

The door snapped shut behind Homel. Contway looked at the door, looked at Homel, and began laughing uproariously. He walked away, leaving Homel to his dilemma.

Bing!

It was the elevator down the hall, about to stop on Homel's floor. The Tiger trainer turned and ran to the end of the hallway. He found an open door. It was a broom closet. He quickly slipped inside. All it contained was a sink and a couple of mops standing against the wall. He noticed a small washcloth draped over the sink and tried to cover himself with the washcloth as much as possible. He opened the door a crack and whenever people walked by, he'd try to get their attention.

"Psssssst," he would say, hoping they'd stop to help him.

He tried this four or five times, but each time people saw a naked man peeking out of the broom closet with a washcloth in front of him, they took off for their rooms and locked the door.

One hour later, a man stopped, understood Homel's dilemma, and went downstairs to get a key to Homel's room. He brought Homel a pair of pants. It is not known what Homel said to Frank Contway the next day. Or if in fact he ever spoke to him again.

Steve Bilko, a hulking first baseman, spent one year with the Tigers, in 1960. He tried to keep his weight down by taking "steamers" in his hotel room. A "steamer" consisted of sitting in the bathroom with towels stuffed under the door and around the windows, and turning on all the hot water faucets.

Another character from that era was J. W. Porter, the freckled-faced catcher. Like Bilko, he liked to eat. He liked to eat a lot. He would walk into a diner and ask for "two dozen over light" and eat all twenty-four eggs at one sitting.

One year Porter was given a subpoena to appear in a New York court on a paternity charge. A woman in Buffalo, New York, claimed he was the father of her baby. Porter talked about it quite openly. He did not seem embarrassed—perhaps it was the poet in him. In addition to playing baseball, he liked to write verse.

Shortly after the paternity charge was filed, Don Wolfe of the *Toledo Blade* interviewed Porter about his penchant for poetry. Wolfe started his story with a limerick:

"While the other players are down in the lobby,

"Porter is in his room, practicing his hobby."

J. W. was always a newsmaker. He lived in Oregon and decided to drive to spring training with his family one year. He drove down the Pacific coast and cut across Arizona, stopping to see the Cleveland Indians, who were training in Tucson. He said hello to everyone and continued his cross-country trek. When he reached Ocala, Florida, just north of Lakeland, he turned on the car radio to catch the sports news. The announcer said the Tigers had just completed a four-player trade with the Cleveland Indians, sending catcher J. W. Porter and pitcher Hal Woodeshick to the Indians for pitcher Hank Aguirre and catcher Jim Hegan. Porter simply made a U-turn and headed back to the Indians' base in Tucson.

Aguirre was yet another happy-go-lucky Tigers player. He was the world's worst hitter, once going 2-for-75. The baseball writers of Detroit gave him the MHH Award—Most Horrible Hitter—a miniature bat with a dozen holes drilled in it.

Aguirre pitched before the big-money era in baseball. He set the record for the smallest pay raise in history: one cent.

When General Manager Jim Campbell wanted to give him the same contract two years in a row, Aguirre told Campbell he had to have a raise—even a penny—because he was a man of pride. Campbell obliged and gave him the one-cent raise.

The Tigers probably had as many flaky players as any team in the history of the game. Steve Boros, a third baseman from the early 1960s, would sit in front of his locker before a game, working his feet around in a box of sand in order to strengthen his ankles. Rocky Bridges, a utility man in 1959–60, got into a milking contest before a game and said the only reason he didn't win is that he said he didn't want to get emotionally involved with the cow. Rocky Colavito got so mad when the fans laughed at a play he made in left field that he threw the ball over the right field roof. Stan Papi, another utility infielder, asked the writers not to print his salary because it was so small he was ashamed. Outfielder Dick Sharon opened his mail one day and got a request for six autographs. The writer told him: "That's how many I need to get one Bill Freehan." Pitcher Dave Tobik's wife was a sportswriter and lasted longer in the big leagues than he did.

And then we had Richie Hebner, the celebrated gravedigger. A third baseman–first baseman, Hebner played for the Tigers in the summers of 1980–81–82 and dug graves for his father in the winters of 1980–81–82. It was hard to say which profession he liked better.

"I'm pretty good at digging graves," said Hebner. "In ten years, no one has ever dug himself out of one yet."

"I hate Forest Lawn," he said. "It's the absolute worst. Those guys dig in tuxedos."

Finally: "I love my father's six graveyards back home. They're

Hank Aguirre was a very capable pitcher and an awful hitter. His lifetime batting average over 16 seasons was a paltry .085. In 1962 he led the league with a 2.21 e.r.a. and batted an anemic .027. ◆

Richie Hebner gave Detroit one fine year in 1980 as he filled in at first base, third, and DH with a .290 average. ♦

great places to dig, except when it gets cold. Then you've got to chip away at the ice. But a good Designated Digger can always get the job done."

And, perhaps the flakiest of them all, a man who took the city by storm with his wild and wonderful ways, a man who was the favorite of young and old alike, a man who captured the hearts of everyone in the game of baseball . . . the one, the only, the original: Mark "The Bird" Fidrych.

You couldn't get near his locker: too many cakes, cookies, flowers, presents, pictures, and stacks of mail in the way.

Ty Cobb? Hank Greenberg? Charlie Gehringer? Mickey Cochrane? Al Kaline? Mickey Lolich? Denny McLain? Alan Trammell? No one was more popular than The Bird, and how long did he last in Detroit? Just 48 games. Twenty-nine wins, nineteen losses. He played parts of five years (1976–80) and was gone. But he was an original. A unique talent with a unique personality.

He talked to the baseball and they all loved him. They loved him beyond belief. No player in Detroit history has been responsible for drawing more people into the ballpark in one season than Mark Fidrych in 1976. He came out of nowhere and from June 1 on, he won 19 games, losing only nine. But more than that, he was a fresh face on the scene—a free spirit who turned the whole town on with his almost unbelievable enthusiasm.

You could actually see him conversing with the ball: "Get down, ball. Get down. Stay low. Stay low, ball." He flailed his arms when he pitched and stomped around on the mound like . . . well, like Big Bird on *Sesame Street*. He applauded his fielders for every play, raced on and off the field, and wouldn't let the groundskeepers make repairs on his mound. He would pat the dirt down. He would smooth it. He would make the dirt feel good.

"When I'm out there, the mound belongs to me," he said.

Yes, indeed.

One night, under a clear moon in Lakeland, he told a young woman he was going to take her to the most beautiful spot on earth. He took her out to the pitcher's mound in Marchant Stadium, training site of the Tigers, where he, uh, well, er . . . yes, he really did it.

Four months—June, July, August, and September of 1976—he flashed across the sky of Detroit. That was all. But he touched people in ways they had never been touched before.

Where the Tigers normally drew 15,000, they would get 40,000 if Fidrych was pitching. Other teams asked weeks in advance for the Detroit pitching rotation so they could hype Fidrych's appearance in their own ballparks.

The Bird showed up in Detroit at exactly the right time. The city was down on its luck and looking for a lift. The economy was suffering and the automotive industry was under siege from the Japanese car builders. Interest rates were up and spirits were down. Suddenly, here was a breath of fresh air at the ballpark. A fuzzy-haired kid talking to the ball and getting them all out. He gave the fans a reason to feel good. He brought them joy. He brought them pleasure. He brought them happiness. They took to him as if he were their own. The love affair burned all through the summer, and then, suddenly, it all came to an end.

The following spring, Fidrych reported to camp with the Tigers and seemed more fidgety than ever. How could he ever top his fantastic 1976 season? He had started the All-Star game, and met the President of the United States. The moment he showed up on the field in Lakeland, he was leaping over fences, jumping up and down, and racing around like a young colt. It was almost as if he were saying, "I'm still the same guy, world. Do you still love me?"

One day, while jumping for a fly ball he should never have jumped for, Fidrych damaged his knee. He underwent surgery, but was never the same again. The whole town prayed for his recovery. The Tigers stuck with him four more years, but he could never get it back. Talking to the ball wasn't enough anymore. When he threw it, it was too slow and too straight. He returned to his farm in Massachusetts, got married, and raised horses and pigs.

In later years, he would say, "I had more than I ever expected and I did the best I could. Everyone was good to me. What more could anyone ask?"

No more, Bird. The memories linger on . . .

Mark the Bird sent Detroit hearts soaring with his astonishing pitching; a rookie season of 19–9 with a league-leading e.r.a. of 2.34. Only a year later, he struggled to 6–4 with a sore arm, and in the last four years of his career, which ended in 1980, he only started 27 games. ♦

SCRAPBOOK

"I was in the outfield, playin' the outfield, right? And then—this is what he [Scout Joe Cusick] told me, when he saw me. He goes, you were out in the outfield . . . I remember the play and everything. The pitcher got wild, and the coach called me in from the outfield. And I had—there was nothin' on the batter, right? I got in there, warmed up, threw one pitch, and the guy swung at it and grounded out to the second baseman. I got the inning over and then went back to the bench. And I went back out to left field and the other guy went back to pitchin' again. And that's all he [Joe Cusick] saw me throw. And he saw me play the outfield. And he signed me—he signed me as a pitcher. But he said he heard from other scouts that, y'know, I was a good pitcher."

Mark Fidrych and Tom Clark, *No Big Deal*

◆

"Fidrych was the greatest thing that came along in baseball at that time. After he hurt his arm I got mail saying I over-pitched him. I never overpitched him one inning in his whole life. I protected that kid. When you have something like that come along you guard it with your life. He could throw the ball in an area this small, one pitch after the other. The ball would just naturally sink, and he would put it right in there, over and over again."

Ralph Houk with Robert W. Creamer, *Season of Glory*

◆

"When, at one point, the Tigers proposed to send him [Boots Poffenberger] to the minors for a period but wanted him to go to Montreal, which was in a faster league than Beaumont, Boots rebelled. It was Beaumont or nowhere for him. . . . He liked the bright lights, the music and the wine when it was red or any other color. It was generally held, among baseball men and the world at large, that for anyone with these proclivities to demand Beaumont, Texas, when Montreal beckoned was comparable to an art lover's selecting an original drawing of Orphan Annie and Sandy in preference to the *Mona Lisa*."

Art Hill, *I Don't Care If I Never Come Back*

◆

"Well, the pitcher wound up and pitched, and sure enough Schaefer stole second. But I had to stay right where I was, on third, because Nig Clarke, the Cleveland catcher, just held on to the ball. He refused to throw to second, knowing I'd probably make it home if he did.

"So now we had men on second and third. Well, on the next pitch Schaefer yelled, 'Let's try it again!' And with a blood curdling shout he took off like a wild Indian *back to first base*, and dove in headfirst in a cloud of dust. He figured the catcher might throw to first—since he evidently wouldn't throw to second—and then I could come home same as before.

Davy Jones to Lawrence Ritter, *The Glory of Their Times*

◆

MAN IN MOTION

♦

Sparky Anderson. Very visible. Very personable. Very successful. But who in Detroit knew anything about him when he was hired as manager of the Tigers on June 12, 1979?

Anderson had been an outstanding manager in Cincinnati. Some couldn't believe it when the Reds fired him. Sparky himself couldn't believe it. What had he done? He had finished second two years in a row. He had given them the best and when he missed two years in a row, they got rid of him.

It was not very often that such a man was available on the open market. Jim Campbell, the Tiger boss, went right after him. He dumped his own man—Les Moss, who had been a longtime employee of the Tigers, a minor league manager who had been loyal to a fault. Poor Les. He was getting his big chance in the major leagues and Campbell took it from him after only two months. To this day, Campbell says it was the hardest thing he ever had to do in his career in baseball. He knew he was being unfair to Moss. But he also knew he could not pass up the chance to get a man of Anderson's caliber.

Yet, for all of his success at Cincinnati—he finished first five times, got into four World Series and won two of them—for all of his national exposure—Sparky Anderson was pretty much an unknown in Detroit.

We knew he was little. We knew he had white hair. We knew he liked to talk a lot. That was about it, other than the fact that he was known as "Captain Hook" for his penchant for pulling pitchers. Somebody mentioned he was once a used car salesman on the side.

A call went out to Tom Callahan, who is now the sports editor

With the Tigers on the verge of a record for consecutive wins (18), Sparky Anderson shagged grounders in the outfield in Seattle at the beginning of the 1984 season. ♦

The Tigers' beefy brain trust: General Manager Jim Campbell and adviser Rick Ferrell. Campbell, in the majors himself for little more than a cup of coffee, fired pal Les Moss in order to hire Sparky Anderson as manager in 1979. ◆

for *Time* magazine. Tom had worked as a columnist in Cincinnati and knew Anderson as well as anyone in our business.

"What's he like, Tom?"

Callahan said if you could understand and accept one thing about Sparky Anderson, you could get along with him. He said, "He changes his mind almost every day. If you can live with that, you'll be okay. What you have to understand is that when he says something on Monday, he means it. He might say something else on Tuesday, but he means that, too. He drove some of the guys crazy in Cincinnati. But if you know there is no intent on his part to deceive you, you'll get along with him. He's a good man. He cares about people."

A second call went to Bob Stevens, the longtime baseball writer in San Francisco.

"Tell me about Sparky."

"Easy," said Stevens. "I can do it in one sentence. He is the most modest egotist you'll ever meet."

Seldom have two sportswriters called anything more correctly.

Anderson changes his mind more than he changes his socks. "It's crazy," Jim Campbell will tell you. "He'll come up to my office after a game and he'll tell me all the things we have to do. Get rid of this guy, get rid of that guy. He wants to make changes every day. Then he'll drive home, and by the time he gets there, he'll call me at my apartment and tell me something different. We'd better keep this guy and we'd better not lose that guy. I say to him, 'Sparky, why don't you go to sleep and we'll talk about it in the morning.' "

A modest egotist? A perfect description. He is modest, but he is egotistical. He is egotistical, but he is modest. It all works for him.

Sparky Anderson knows he is good. He knows who is he. But he also knows he is the luckiest man in the world to have what he has in life. He appreciates his good fortune and tries to repay it in all the ways that are open to him. He does it mostly by being nice to people. He treats everyone with care and concern. The smallest as well as the biggest get full attention from this man.

He writes a column for my newspaper and gives the money he earns from it to Children's Hospital. He runs an annual auction for the afflicted kids at Children's Hospital and Ford Hospital. Recently he began having an annual dinner for them. He does this with great flair because he believes the more publicity he gets for these charities, the more he can help them. It would be easy to question his motives, but he doesn't care. He knows what he is doing and, more importantly, why he is doing it.

What is not well-publicized is that he is forever visiting the kids in the hospital, taking one of his players or coaches along with him. He deals mostly with terminally ill children—the ones with no hope. He tries to bring them a smile, and maybe a piece of pizza.

"You look like a pepperoni guy to me," he'll say to a small boy confined to a bed.

The boy will manage a weak smile.

"And you," he'll say to the youngster in the next bed, "you look like double cheese."

Few know about these gestures of compassion. Sparky tries to keep things like that quiet. No cameras, please. He just wants to say thank-you in his own way. He is, as Tom Callahan said, a good man.

So what if he runs his mouth too much? So what if he tells you nobody ever played center field the way Chet Lemon played it, or that Matt Nokes is going to be one of the great hitters of modern times, or that Alan Trammell is as good a shortstop as any the game has ever seen.

That is his way.

His enthusiasm is genuine. He wakes up in the morning and can't believe how good the coffee tastes. He can't believe he can sit in the corner of the kitchen for a whole hour sipping coffee and reading the morning papers. It is the good life and he knows

Anderson blows a contemplative bubble as he considers a pitching change during a 1982 game with the Minnesota Twins. ◆

it, and he can't help himself for feeling 'up' all the time. You might see him tired once or twice a season, but that's all.

Small? White haired? Talkative? He is all of these things, but more than that, he is a warm and caring man. He knows it is more important to tell the truth than to win pennants. Pennants pass; the truth lives forever.

He is simply a man of high standards.

Would you like to hear some of his wit and wisdom? He never got past high school. He is not a learned man. He doesn't read books or listen to music. He doesn't go to museums. His best times are spent sitting at home in his jogging suit eating a tuna fish sandwich and watching a basketball game on ESPN. Make that nine basketball games on ESPN.

But listen:

- "The easiest thing in the world to do is manage a team that's winning. Anyone can do it. Your players are in a great frame of mind and you can talk to them and tell them all the things you want. They believe everything you say. Losing, now that's different. They're down. The pressure is on them. They're thinking of themselves, not the team. That's when you find out who you can depend on and who you can't."
- "If there is anything that bothers me about newspapers, it's the 'unnamed source.' When I read about an 'unnamed source,' I don't trust the writer. If you can't put a name to your comments, the comments aren't worth anything."
- "The biggest mistake people make is when they bad-mouth

Umpire Ken Kaiser rejected Anderson's protest over a decision to call time out when Tiger Darrell Evans bumped into Minnesota Twin Kent Hrbek. The pause nullified a Detroit run. ◆

people when they're fired. Once you bad-mouth people, you can't bring it back."

- "Umpires are so much more right than we are, it's unbelievable."
- "If I wasn't a manager, I would have been a house painter. I like to paint. I'm a good painter. You can't get in trouble when you paint. If you see something wrong, you just paint over it."
- "The only thing a manager can do once the game starts is to make moves with his pitchers, and you're going to be good at that only if you have good pitchers."
- "I understand people who boo us. It's like going to a Broadway show. You pay for your tickets and expect to be entertained. When you're not, you have a right to complain."
- "I like to see other managers happy when they win because I know what the feeling is."
- "The reason I keep my head down when I come back from the mound after changing pitchers is because the guy who is screaming at me might be my neighbor and I don't want to know it."
- "I can't believe they pay us for this—something we did for nothing as kids."

The 1989 season marks Anderson's twentieth year as a major league manager. He has been the most successful manager in the American League in the 1980s. He has won one pennant, a World Series, and two divisional titles. After eleven seasons in Detroit, he has become the most dominant figure on the Tigers. He is the unquestioned leader of this team.

You want something, you go to Sparky. A question. An answer. A little baseball talk. It's always there, always dispensed with a care and concern you don't usually find in managerial offices. You can talk to him when he loses. In fact, he talks better after he loses than after he wins. He always takes losing as a personal challenge and he is a man who forever likes challenges. He likes to prove he can handle adversity.

This is a man who is not afraid to reveal his feelings.

"I never thought there was such a thing as getting old," he said. "When you are young, nothing bothers you. You think you are special. You think life will go on forever. Then, one day, while you're playing a round of golf or just working around the yard, you get this twinge in your shoulder or your thumb feels a little sore and you wonder what's going on. You realize that you're not so special after all. You realize you are given only so many days on this earth and you'd better not throw any of them away."

At the age of fifty-five, George Lee Anderson lives life to the fullest.

Here's Sparky during the last few days of the 1984 season:

Sunday Afternoon

He hears the fans clamoring, calling out his name as he starts up the tunnel to the clubhouse.

"Sparky! Sparky! Sparky!"

His team has just clinched the division and they are asking him to come back out on the field. He feels a rush of embarrassment but stops in his tracks.

"Sparky! Sparky! Sparky!"

He turns around and bounces up the dugout steps. He faces the stands and doffs his cap. The roars get louder. Then he goes down the steps and is gone from sight. Nobody notices, but there is no smile on his face.

Sunday Night

It is two hours later and Sparky is sitting in Armando's restaurant near the ballpark. He is with his wife, Carol, his son, Al, and his coach, Billy Consolo. Consolo is Sparky's best friend and is living with him in Sparky's house in Bloomfield Hills.

Sparky says to his son, "Hey, Al, were you cheering for me like everyone else?"

The young man stirs in his chair.

His mother says, "Yes, he was standing like everyone else. He was applauding like everyone else. When he realized they were calling out *your* name, he stopped applauding and sat down."

Sparky laughs.

"That's my son," he says. "A man of taste."

Sparky orders a chicken taco and cheese enchilada. They are his favorites. He also orders a steak, cooked in lemon and garlic and covered with onions. "This is heaven," he says.

The owner comes by the table. "This one is on the players," he says. "They just called up and want to pick up the check."

Sparky wipes his mouth and looks from over the top of his napkin.

"Thank you, my man," he says. "I thank you for your thought. But I have been around the block a few times. You put that check right down here and I will take care of it."

The owner looks at him and smiles.

Monday Morning

Sparky knows the phone will ring at about 7:40. That's when J. P. McCarthy of radio station WJR will be calling. He calls

Coach Billy Consolo spent ten seasons as a utility infielder with six different teams between 1953 and 1962. ♦

almost every morning to chat with the Detroit manager.

Sparky pulls his thoughts together and is ready when the phone rings. They talk for five minutes. He hangs up and lights his pipe. He lies back on the pillow and looks up at the ceiling. Nice ceiling, he thinks. Good paint job.

He drives to the ballpark with Consolo. He goes up to Jim Campbell's office. Campbell is sitting behind his desk. Sparky walks in and says, "How'd you like what those fans did yesterday, giving me that big ovation?"

"Not bad," says Campbell.

"What I should have done," says Sparky, "is gone out to the middle of the mound and raised my hands like Julius Caesar and let them really get a look at me. I mean, that's a great body they were seeing out there yesterday."

Campbell tells Sparky he'd better not miss the bus to the airport.

Monday Afternoon

Sparky is first off the team bus when it arrives at the hotel in Milwaukee. He walks into the lobby, where they've got coffee, soda pop, milk, and cookies set out for the team's arrival.

He picks up a couple of cans of Coke and two cookies and heads for his room. He figures they will make a nice snack after the game. One hour later the cookies are gone.

Another argument falls on deaf ears; this time Umpire Jerry Neudecker ignores Anderson's reasoning. ◆

Tuesday Morning

It is nine o'clock and Sparky is sitting in the corner booth of the coffee shop. He is wearing his jogging suit. It is raining.

Don Sutton, then a Milwaukee pitcher, sits down at the next table.

"You ever see lightning like that last night?" Sutton says.

"I think one bolt hit the loudspeakers," says Sparky. "It was the second loudest noise I ever heard in a ballpark."

Sutton stares at him.

"You're not going to believe the first," Sparky says. "It happened in Dodger Stadium. 1970. I'm with the Reds and Woody Woodward is our shortstop. He's standing out there and—BAM!—this puff of smoke goes right up in the air, right behind him, and we all just about jump out of our uniforms from the noise. Do you know what it was?"

Sutton is still staring.

"It was a bag of flour," says Sparky. "A BAG OF FLOUR! Somebody had dropped the thing from an airplane and if it lands on Woodward, I mean he's gone. It kills him."

Tuesday Afternoon

Back in his room, Sparky turns on his TV set. He watches a replay of the Boston College–North Carolina football game. He doesn't like what he sees. Doug Flutie has four touchdown passes for Boston College. His coach keeps him on the field and pretty soon he has six touchdown passes.

Sparky turns off the TV set. He thinks to himself, "The Heisman Trophy, eh? Is that how they do it—they rub it in."

Sparky picks up the phone. He dials Detroit. He is checking in with "The King." That's what he calls Jim Campbell.

He says, "Hey, King, this is The Slob calling."

Campbell laughs. They talk about the team for about fifteen minutes, then Sparky heads out to the ballpark.

Marty Castillo, a utility infielder, asks if Sparky and his coaches will leave the clubhouse for a while. They want to talk over how to cut up their World Series shares.

"May I say a few words to the boys before I leave?" Sparky asks. Castillo nods.

"Thank you," says Sparky.

The Detroit manager makes sure the dressing room door is closed. He gets the attention of his players. "You guys do what you want but I just want you to know how Johnny Bench handled things in Cincinnati," Sparky says. "He'd tell all the guys, 'Hey, men, this is free money. Let's make sure we share it with everybody.' "

Sparky walks out of the room. It is silent as he leaves.

Wednesday Morning

It is 11:45 and the AP photographer raps on the door of Sparky's hotel room in midtown Manhattan. He is there to do a picture story on the Detroit manager.

Sparky opens the door. "Come in, come in," he says to the photographer.

The room is small, just a bed, a dresser, and a couple of chairs. It is not what the photographer wanted to see. He needs a little room to do his work.

A phone rings somewhere in the distance.

"Man, there it goes again," says Sparky. "That guy next door has sure been getting a lot of calls." The phone is ringing and ringing.

The photographer tries the door beween the rooms. It opens. He pokes his head in and sees a luxurious layout—sofas, easy chairs, drapes, two TV sets, a small dining room. A tray of sandwiches and a bowl of fruit are set out on the table. A magnum of champagne is sitting in a silver bucket.

"I think this is for you," says the photographer.

Sparky peeks in. "I'll be damned," he says. "I didn't know I had two rooms."

Wednesday Night

It is almost midnight when the bus gets back to the hotel. Everyone gets off except one man. When they're all gone, Sparky says to the bus driver: "Okay, Josh, you know where to go."

The driver nods and pulls away into the night. Ten minutes later he stops in front of the Stage Deli. Sparky bows to him before he gets out. "Thank you, my man. I will see you tomorrow night."

The driver salutes him.

Sparky goes inside where two of his coaches—Consolo and Dick Tracewski—are waiting for him.

He orders a liverwurst sandwich on rye. He always orders a liverwurst sandwich on rye at the Stage Deli. They sit there until two o'clock in the morning, talking baseball.

These are but a few days in the life of this man—but they are typical of his life-style. He lives from morning to night, and sometimes, in the middle of the night, he'll get up and write out a new lineup. He loves his life and wants it to go on forever.

The 1989 season is his eleventh year in Detroit. He won 100 games in the National League and now he has won 100 games in the American League. No other manager in history has ever accomplished that feat. He has also won a World Series in the National League and a World Series in the American League. No one has ever done that, either.

S C R A P B O O K

"In yesterday's *Detroit Free Press*, an article about Sparky Anderson . . . described him as the kind of man you wish your father had been. That is not to be read as a criticism of fathers. I'm one myself. But few of us are (or had) fathers as downright wonderful as Sparky. He is decent, warm, generous, kind, fiercely loyal. Just about everything you'd want in a father. Or a son."

> Art Hill, *I Don't Care If I Never Come Back*

◆

"Sparky communicates well. He's intelligent. He has the 'smarts.' He believes in his convictions. He'll argue to the death when he thinks he's right. And usually he is right.

"He puts the needle in very well. He really amuses me at times but I have acquired great respect for him."

> Tom Seaver to Sparky Anderson and Si Burick, *The Main Spark*

◆

"It is really hot and Dan Petry is starting to struggle in the ninth inning. I walk out to talk to him. 'It must be a hundred degrees out here,' I say. 'Yep,' Petry answers. 'It sure is hot," I say. 'Yep,' says Petry. 'You've thrown a lot of pitches. How do you feel?' I say. 'How do you think I feel?' he says. 'Well, you're going to feel a lot worse, because you're leaving.' "

> Sparky Anderson's personal diary, July 22, 1984

"I refuse to call a forty-seven-year-old man Sparky."

> Umpire Al Clark on why he addresses Anderson as "George."

◆

"Sparky came here two years ago promising to build a team in his own image and now the club is looking for small, white-haired infielders with .212 batting averages."

> Tiger announcer Al Ackerman in 1981

◆

"He talks a lot on the bench. When he gets keyed up he talks, talks, talks. He's a bit of a politician, not that he intends to be, or that he'd deliberately hurt anyone. He believes in certain principles and in certain people. And he makes it a point not to offend anyone.

"You can kid him, and he doesn't mind. Sometimes I call him 'John McGraw' because he makes so many moves. Pitcher, infielder, outfielder, he'll switch guys in a close game; always he's two or three innings ahead, and I guess that's part of the reason for his success."

> Johnny Bench to Sparky Anderson and Si Burick, *The Main Spark*

◆

He talks about managing the Tigers longer than anyone in history. Hughie Jennings holds the mark with fourteen years. Sparky is closing in on him. He knows it will be difficult to last fourteen years in Detroit because his boss—The King—Jim Campbell—is at retirement age and is getting ready to ease himself out of the picture. Campbell has been Sparky's greatest supporter. If firing Moss was the toughest thing Campbell ever had to do, hiring Sparky Anderson was the best thing he ever did.

"It's going to be tough to hang around," says Sparky. "I know you can wear out your welcome, no matter how well you may do your job. They just get tired of you. They've heard all your stories and seen all your stuff—they know your whole act—and they want something different. They want something new. It's unavoidable. I'm flattered I've lasted this long."

Sparky and his wife Carol have been married for more than thirty-five years. He explains why his marriage works.

"Carol gives me my freedom," he says. "She allows me to do my job. In all these years of traveling, she has called me only four times on the road and I remember them all. She called me in Philadelphia in 1959. Our oldest boy, Lee, had a temperature—107—and they had to put him into an ice tube, and Carol was frightened. She called me when Lee was going to get married in Las Vegas. That was in 1976. She called me when Lefty Phillips died. He was my closest friend. That was in 1975. And she called me when our son, Albert, was in a car accident in 1983."

It is clear Anderson cares for his wife.

He says, "I'd rather be with her than anyone else. She is my best friend. She is always correcting me, telling me when I'm running my mouth too much. And you know me, I'm always running my mouth. I am really an introvert. I'm a very shy person. When the season is on, I am Sparky Anderson. When it's over, I am George Anderson. Very few people know George Anderson."

This is true, but a lot of Tiger fans know Sparky and like what he's done with their ball club in his years at the helm.

Another time, another place, another life as the Cincinnati Reds embrace the Sparky Anderson who managed them to the 1975 championship win. ♦

BLESS YOU, BOYS

◆

Under Jim Campbell's direction, the Tigers developed the core of the 1968 championship team. They produced such promising players as Willie Horton, Mickey Stanley, Jim Northrup, Bill Freehan, Gates Brown, Dick McAuliffe, Don Wert, Mickey Lolich, and Joe Sparma. These youngsters blended in with such older hands as Al Kaline and Norm Cash, plus the brash young kid from Chicago—Dennis Dale McLain—and Earl Wilson, the veteran pitcher from Boston. The arrival of Wilson in Detroit was a signal event because he brought with him the first agent in baseball history—Bob Woolf, the Boston attorney.

"It was almost comical," said Wilson of his dealings with Campbell. "I'd ask for something and Campbell would make an offer. I'd run to the phone in the next room and call Woolf at his hotel room in downtown Detroit and tell him what Campbell said. He'd tell me to ask for something else. I kept going out of Campbell's office so much, he must have thought I had an upset stomach and was going to the bathroom."

Where Campbell made a mistake is that he stayed too long with his 1968 champions. He let them get old on him. Billy Martin was able to coax one more season out of them in 1972. The club won the AL East but dropped the playoff to Oakland. After that the Detroit ball club all but disintegrated. For the rest of the decade, the Tigers finished third, sixth, sixth, fifth, fourth, fifth, fifth, losing a record nineteen games in a row in 1975.

During this time, the Tigers saw relief ace John Hiller suffer a heart attack and then come back and pitch more brilliantly than ever. They also signed a player out of Jackson Prison, Ron LeFlore, and he became an outstanding base stealer and fixture

By 1970, Al Kaline was 36 years old and confronting an inevitable erosion of skills. However he refused to surrender quickly, hitting .294 in 1971 and then .313 in an injury-shortened season a year later. His statistics for 1972 included a blazing 10 for 24 as a pinch hitter, a .416 average. He retired in 1974 on the cusp of his fortieth birthday. ◆

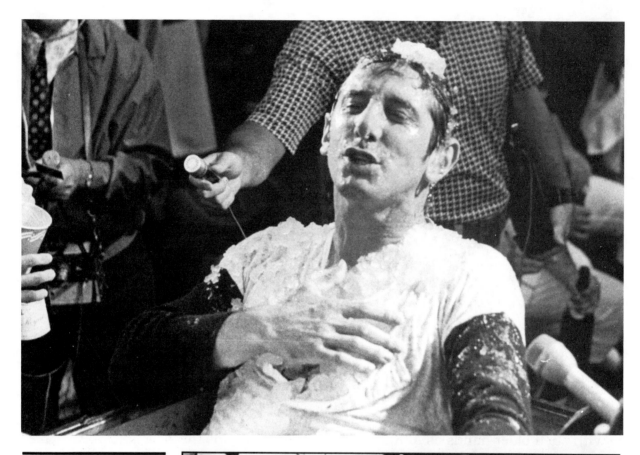

Manager Billy Martin, encased in celebratory ice, holds court after the Tigers clinched the American League East in 1972. The Martin-led Tigers lost in the playoffs to Dick Williams' Oakland A's. ◆

Ron LeFlore brought the excitement of base stealing to town with his debut in 1974. In his four best seasons for the Tigers, 1976–79, he averaged well over .300 and stole a total of 243 bases. ◆

in center field for the rest of the 1970s. LeFlore was an exciting performer when he put his mind to it. But Campbell eventually dumped him because he didn't like his off-the-field behavior.

Campbell knew he had to rebuild the whole team, so he bought himself some time by bringing in Ralph Houk, a steady hand, to manage the team from 1974 through 1978. Houk served him well in those five years—not winning anything, but showing the patience that was needed as the Tigers started developing a whole new set of young players.

The new heroes started coming out of the minors in 1977 with the appearance of pitcher Jack Morris. Alan Trammell, Lou Whitaker, and Lance Parrish arrived in 1978. Tom Brookens in 1979. Kirk Gibson and Dan Petry in 1980.

After Houk grew tired of the task, Campbell made another astute move by bringing in Sparky Anderson to manage the team in 1979. Campbell was passing the team on from one veteran manager to another, but he still wasn't done. He named Bill Lajoie his chief scout in 1974 and promoted him to director of player procurement in 1975. Lajoie knew the business of talent and, in 1983, Campbell named him the general manager of the Tigers. He gave Lajoie as much free rein as Fetzer had given him,

Alan Trammell watches the first of his two homers clear the fence in World Series Game 4, 1984. Trammell drove in all four runs for Detroit in the victory. He hit .314 for the year, .450 in the Series, and .364 in the play-offs. ◆

Kirk Gibson leaps to steal a homer from Oriole Rick Dempsey, who would become his teammate on the 1988 champion Los Angeles Dodgers. In the '84 Series, Gibson saved a win when he threw out Curt Bevaqua trying to stretch a double into a triple. ◆

Mickey Lolich became the top Tigers pitcher after his three wins in the 1968 World Series, a 19-victory season in 1969, a slip to 14–19 in '70, and then 25 and 22 wins in the next two years. Altogether he gave the club 207 regular season triumphs before finishing out his years with the Mets and finally San Diego in 1979. ◆

and it was Lajoie who produced the 1984 champions—the "Bless You, Boys" gang that won 35 of their first 40 games, clinched the division, stomped on Kansas City in the play-offs, and ran over San Diego in the World Series.

It was some season, 1984. The motto—"Bless You, Boys"—came from one of Campbell's greatest critics: Detroit telecaster Al Ackerman. Big Al climbed on the bandwagon when the Tigers started winning in 1984. In fact, he rode in the victory parade after the season was over. Later on, Big Al said it was a mistake to ride in the parade. He did not want to be labeled a fan and, worse, a front-runner. He liked to play the role of an independent.

Campbell would get furious with Big Al. The commentator used to call Campbell a cheapskate and do it on the 11:00 news. He called him other things, too. Campbell wanted to shoot back, but Fetzer interceded and gave Campbell some of the best advice he ever got in his life.

Fetzer called Campbell aside and told him, "In your position as President of the Tigers, you don't have the luxury to war with the media."

Others noticed that Campbell took all of their brickbats, so they kept hurling them at him, never understanding why he didn't throw them back.

Lou Whitaker slides in for a score while Milwaukee catcher Bill Schroeder squats for a throw that never arrived. ♦

Entrepreneur Thomas Monaghan built his pizza business into a national empire and became one of America's wealthiest men. In his first year as owner of the Tigers, the club brought him a World Series championship. ◆

Anyway, Big Al was allowed to ride in the parade. Nobody minded it, least of all the fans. It had been an exhilarating season for them and they were pleased with Big Al because he was the one who gave them their battle cry in 1984—"Bless You, Boys."

Sparky Anderson had a terrific time for himself in 1984. He got what he wanted more than anything else. He won a World Championship in another city, showing the people who fired him in Cincinnati in 1978 that they had made a grave mistake. Sparky never talked about it because he is a smart man. But that's what 1984 meant to him: vindication.

Sparky was so taken by what went on during the season that he wrote a book about it. It was a daily diary and sold over 100,000 copies. He called it—you got it—*Bless You, Boys*.

By now, the club had a new owner—Tom Monaghan, the pizza entrepreneur who bought the Tigers from the aging Fetzer in the autumn of 1983. He paid $53 million and asked Fetzer to stay on as chairman of the board. He also signed Campbell to a five-year contract as his president and chief executive officer. Monaghan, who was forty-five at the time, sat back and went along for the ride. He enjoyed every moment as his team frolicked through the season.

Campbell, as always, was loyal to his boss. He started sending his weekly reports to Monaghan at his office in Ann Arbor, Michigan. Monaghan, in turn, left Campbell alone.

It was truly an incredible season. Nobody goes 35–5 at the start of the season, but the Tigers did, and were never out of first place. They led from start to finish. They won 104 games and drew 2,704,794 fans, an all-time record in Detroit. The bandwagon started rolling early and everybody jumped on. Disc jockeys did almost nothing but talk about the Tigers when they weren't playing music. The same happened on the 11:00 news. The anchorpeople thought nothing of stealing the sportscaster's show by giving away the Tigers' score and putting in their two-cents' worth. Everyone wanted to be identified with the Tigers.

Jack Morris pitched a no-hitter on the first Saturday of the season. Seven Tigers reached double digits in home runs. Willie Hernandez, acquired from the Philadelphia Phillies in spring training, was almost a perfect pitcher out of the bull pen. He posted a 9–3 record with 32 saves and won the Most Valuable Player award as well as the Cy Young Award.

Everybody chipped in and the team blended perfectly. The Tigers became an irresistible force, clinching the division early and running over the overmatched Kansas City Royals in three quick games in the playoffs.

The ease with which Detroit captured the American League

flag in 1984 made the club odds-on favorites to chew up its World Series opponent, San Diego. The Padres, by contrast, had squeaked into the fall finale. Their closest competitor in the National League West, Atlanta, finished the season under .500. While Detroit was wiping out Kansas City, San Diego barely survived its play-offs with the Chicago Cubs. The Padres dropped the first two games and then amazed everybody with an unprecedented three straight victories. (In those days league championships were decided in a best of five format.)

In Game 1 of the Series, Jack Morris yielded two quick runs in the first inning and then settled in to shut out San Diego for the next eight innings. Larry Herndon came through with a two-run homer in the fifth to give the Tigers the edge. The National Leaguers had one chance to tie in the seventh when leadoff hitter Curt Bevaqua hammered a ball past Kirk Gibson. Bevaqua rounded second and sprinted for third. Meanwhile, Gibson came up with the ball and fired it toward the bag. The throw beat the runner and instead of a man in scoring position with none out, San Diego had nobody aboard and one out.

In Game 2, Dan Petry (18–8 in the regular season) gave up early single runs and then, with two on, Bevaqua homered for a 5–3 San Diego victory. But after that, the National Leaguers were beyond prayer. In Game 3 the Padre pitchers walked 11 men; the Tigers collected only 7 hits and won 5–2, leaving 14 men on base.

The championship club of 1984 broke out of the gate with an extended winning streak and coasted to the pennant. ◆

Game 4 was The Alan Trammell Show. The shortstop belted a pair of two-run homers, which was more than enough for Jack Morris, who again allowed just two runs as he won 4–2. Kirk Gibson strutted to center stage in Game 5, where his two homers knocked in five runs, and Petry triumphed 8–4.

It was not a pretty World Series, or a particularly dramatic one. But the Tigers, for the first time in sixteen years, stood at the pinnacle of the baseball world.

Nothing, however, stays the same in this game of baseball. Consider what's happened to the 1984 champions in Detroit. As the team prepares for the 1989 season, only seven players are left from the '84 squad, and one of those has changed his name. It's not Willie Hernandez anymore, but *Guillermo* Hernandez. He feels he can pitch better if he is called by his proper name, and who is to argue with him?

Hernandez is one of only two pitchers left from the '84 team.

Among the others, only four remain—shortstop Alan Trammell, second baseman Lou Whitaker, outfielder Chet Lemon, and first baseman Dave Bergman.

The Tigers enter 1990 in another transition period, faced with another rebuilding process. What complicates matters for them is that they are facing some changes in top management. John Fetzer is 89 and all but out of the picture. Jim Campbell will turn 66 in 1990 and has built himself new homes in Dearborn and Lakeland, Florida, in preparation for his retirement. Campbell has spoken alternately about not hanging around too long and about remaining in some type of advisory capacity. He has been in control of the Tigers for more than 25 years and will be sorely missed when he leaves. He led the Tigers to two divisional titles and two World Series titles, while also serving as

Pitcher Jack Morris opened the 1984 Series with a 3–2 win and celebrated on the mound with first baseman Dave Bergman and catcher Lance Parrish. Morris came back to top San Diego 4–2 in Game 4. ◆

Monaghan's creation, Domino's Pizza keeps its pies warm for delivery with special trucks. The owner warmed hearts in the press box in the 1984 Series with a special delivery by helicopter. ◆

The Tiger squad tears from the dugout after the final out of the 1984 Series. ◆

High fives from Alan Trammell and Lance Parrish attend Kirk Gibson's homer with two on in the eighth inning of Game 5 of the 1984 World Series against San Diego. Gibson drove in two more runs with another four-bagger to lead his club to the final victory as the Tigers knocked off the Padres in five games. ◆

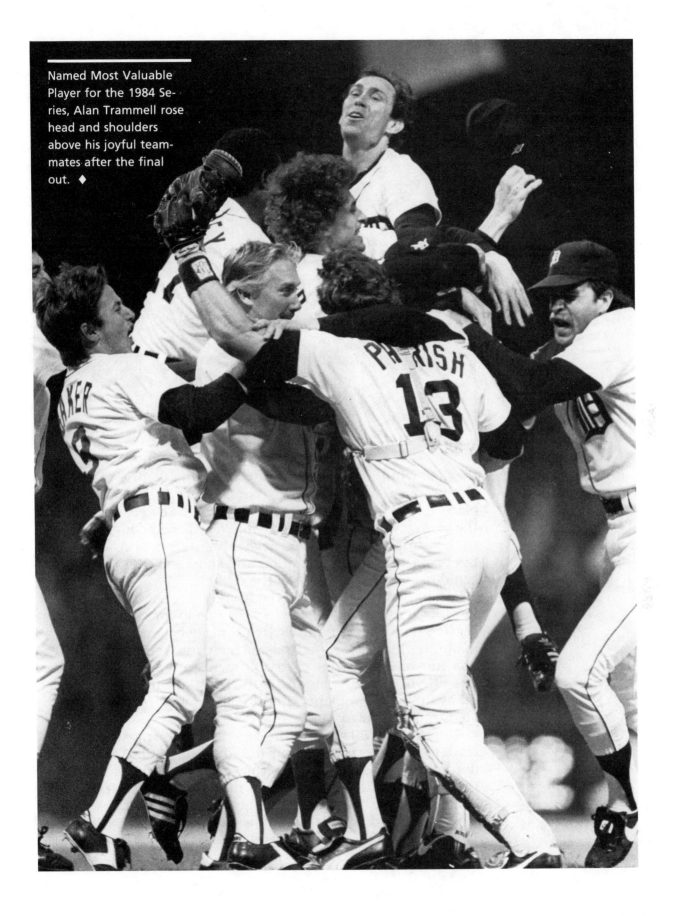

Named Most Valuable Player for the 1984 Series, Alan Trammell rose head and shoulders above his joyful teammates after the final out. ◆

Lefty Frank Tanana clinched the American League East for Detroit in 1987 with a 1–0 shut-out. But a surprising Minnesota club upset the Tigers in the league series. ◆

the steadying influence through the difficult times. His hide has proven to be very thick. Who knows who could take his place? Monaghan has stayed away from the direct operation of the team and does not seem inclined to become more involved in the future. His daughter, Susie, has been working in many facets of the baseball operation and some feel that one day she could be named president of the club.

In addition to revamping the front office, the Tigers face the need for a new place to play as they head for the twenty-first century. The day is coming when some decision will have to be made on whether to pour millions more into refurbishing Tiger Stadium one more time or to put up an entirely new structure. The city of Detroit holds title to the stadium, but it has so many financial problems that it could not think of building a stadium on its own.

Entering the '89 season, the Tigers were the most successful team in the American League during the 1980s. Through the first nine years of the decade, they won more games than even the New York Yankees. It was a mark Sparky Anderson was justly proud of, because he had been there the whole time.

So, too, had Morris, Trammell, Whitaker, and Brookens. These four could truly be called the heart of the Tigers.

Morris is a workhorse. He almost never missed a turn all

Neck cords bulging, glove flapped over on his left hand, Jack Morris fires toward home in Game 4 of the 1987 American League Championship Series. Morris was 19–11 over the regular season and also won a play-off game against Kansas City. ◆

(Left) Trammell and Baltimore Oriole Len Sakata peer at first to see whether the Tigers have turned another dp. (Right) Trammell steals second with a headfirst slide against Oakland. A consistent double-digit thief, Trammell's best was 30 in 1983. ◆

Trammell points to Gibson just before the start of the 1987 American League Playoff Series. A year later, Gibson wore Dodger blue and his timely homer catapulted Los Angeles into the World Series. ◆

through the decade. It wasn't easy for him because he had to fight his own temper as well as the enemy batters. He did an excellent job of conquering both. His best year was 1986, when he went 21 and 8. He also won twenty games (20–13) in 1983. Nobody has appreciated Morris more than his manager. Sparky Anderson knew that no matter what was wrong with his ball club, Morris would stand ready to pitch for him. Morris, a temperamental type, would go into some awful streaks where he almost seemed to forget how to pitch, but he always fought through his problems, mental as well as physical. One reason for his success was physical conditioning. Morris always kept himself in shape and he did it without a fuss. He was very businesslike in his approach to baseball, though those who know him best would tell you he is such a competitor that he would play the game for nothing.

Trammell has been another shining light all through the 1980s—another player the Tigers were able to depend on. He was the steadiest player of all, both on and off the field. He was the one player who had the admiration of everyone in his profession. No one ever had a harsh word for Alan, who never complained, never alibied, and was courteous to everyone. He also knew how to play the game.

Trammell fought some nerves through the early years. He felt strange on the major league scene—almost as if he didn't belong. He kept to himself. They said he would be a great leader one day, but it took time.

He came into his own during the 1984 World Series. He played with a kind of confidence that can only come to someone who finally understands his position in life. Trammell seemed to recognize that he was one of the best players in the game and that settled him down. He no longer had to force himself to do things. He could do them naturally. He could strike out or pop up or kick one in the field and take it in stride, because he knew he would get another chance and it wouldn't happen again.

Trammell batted .364 in the 1984 playoffs and .450 in the World Series, with three home runs in post-season play. He was named the Most Valuable Player of the World Series.

The interesting thing about Trammell is that the more pressure the Tigers put on him, the better he responds. After the club lost catcher Lance Parrish to free agency in 1987, they put Trammell into his cleanup position and Trammell gave them his finest season—a .343 batting average, with 28 homers and 105 RBIs. He finished second to Toronto's George Bell for the Most Valuable Player award.

In 1988, the Tigers asked even more from Trammell. They

Tom Brookens, the third sacker for the Tigers since 1979 loosens up at the Lakeland, Florida, spring training plant. ♦

asked him to make up for the loss of Parish *and* Kirk Gibson. Gibson also left as a free agent, going to the Los Angeles Dodgers. The Tigers were left virtually powerless and Trammell did all he could, batting .311 with 15 homers and 69 RBIs. These were not big numbers, but he was hurt for part of the year, missing an uncharacteristic 34 games. As it turned out, the Tigers finished second, only one game out of the lead. It was, in some ways, a miracle season because the Tigers did it with a sub-par lineup.

Trammell's partner, Lou Whitaker, has also been a consistent performer all through the 1980s. No one fielded his position better, and he was a constant threat at the plate. Whitaker had a below average year in 1988 as he missed 47 games, most of them from hurting his knee in September in a dance-floor incident.

Whitaker stands five eleven and weighs only 160, but he shows surprising power for a man of his size. He has driven the ball great distances, including one shot over the right field roof of Tiger Stadium. Nobody in the game has a better arm than the Detroit second baseman. At times he has been the best player on the team.

The Tigers hit bottom in 1989, finishing in last place with the worst record in baseball: 59 wins and 103 losses. Everything seemed to collapse at once, including manager Sparky Anderson, who suffered from exhaustion and had to return to his home in May for nearly 3 weeks of rest and relaxation. Nothing really worked. The hitters didn't hit, the pitchers didn't pitch, and nobody seemed capable of making the simplest plays. On top of this, the Tigers incurred an inordinate amount of injuries and made several terrible trades. But, as they endured through most of this century, they would endure again. Baseball is such a part of Detroit's culture that the sport may suffer but it will never die.

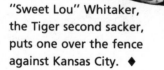

"Sweet Lou" Whitaker, the Tiger second sacker, puts one over the fence against Kansas City. ◆

APPENDICES
TIGER FACTS AND FIGURES

◆

Batting Leaders by Year

Year	Leader in Hits		Leader in HR		Leader in RBI		Leader in AVG	
1901	Barrett	159	Barrett	4	Elberfeld	76	Elberfeld	.310
			Holmes	4				
1902	Barrett	154	Casey	3	Elberfeld	64	Elberfeld	.303
1903	Crawford	184	Crawford	4	Crawford	89	Crawford	.335
1904	Barrett	167	Crawford	2	Crawford	73	Barrett	.268
			Hickman	2				
			McIntyre	2				
1905	Crawford	171	Crawford	6	Crawford	75	Crawford	.297
1906	Crawford	166	Coughlin	2	Crawford	72	Crawford	.295
			Crawford	2				
			O'Leary	2				
			Schaefer	2				
1907	Cobb	212*	Cobb	5	Cobb	116*	Cobb	350*
1908	Cobb	188*	Crawford	7*	Cobb	108*	Cobb	.324*
1909	Cobb	216*	Cobb	9*	Cobb	107*	Cobb	.377*
1910	Cobb	196	Cobb	8	Crawford	120*	Cobb	.385*
1911	Cobb	248*	Cobb	8	Cobb	144*	Cobb	.420*
1912	Cobb	227*	Cobb	7	Crawford	109	Cobb	.410*
1913	Crawford	193	Crawford	9	Crawford	83	Cobb	.390*
1914	Crawford	183	Crawford	8	Crawford	104*	Cobb	.368*
1915	Cobb	208*	Burns	5	Crawford	112†	Cobb	.369*
					Veach	112†		
1916	Cobb	201	Cobb	5	Veach	91	Cobb	.371
1917	Cobb	225*	Veach	8	Veach	103*	Cobb	.383*
1918	Cobb	161	Heilmann	5	Veach	78*	Cobb	.382*
1919	Cobb	191†	Heilmann	8	Veach	101	Cobb	.384*
	Veach	191†						
1920	Veach	188	Veach	11	Veach	113	Cobb	.334
1921	Heilmann	237*	Heilmann	19	Heilmann	139	Heilmann	.394*
1922	Cobb	211	Heilmann	21	Veach	126	Cobb	.401
1923	Heilmann	211	Heilmann	18	Heilmann	115	Heilmann	.403*
1924	Cobb	211	Heilmann	10	Heilmann	113	Heilmann	.346
1925	Heilmann	225	Heilmann	13	Heilmann	133	Heilmann	.393*
1926	Manush	188	Manush	14	Heilmann	103	Manush	.378*
1927	Heilmann	201	Heilmann	14	Heilmann	120	Heilmann	.398*
1928	Gehringer	193	Heilmann	14	Heilmann	107	Heilmann	.328
1929	Alexander	215†	Alexander	25	Alexander	137	Heilmann	.344
	Gehringer	215†						
1930	Gehringer	201	Alexander	20	Alexander	135	Gehringer	.330

*Led league   †Tied for league lead

Year	Leader in Hits		Leader in HR		Leader in RBI		Leader in AVG	
1931	Stone	191	Stone	10	Alexander	87	Stone	.327
1932	Gehringer	184	Gehringer	19	Stone	108	Walker	.323
1933	Gehringer	204	Gehringer	12	Gehringer	105	Gehringer	.325
			Greenberg	12				
1934	Gehringer	214*	Greenberg	26	Greenberg	139	Gehringer	.356
1935	Greenberg	203	Greenberg	36†	Greenberg	170*	Gehringer	.330
1936	Gehringer	227	Goslin	24	Goslin	125	Gehringer	.354
1937	Walker	213	Greenberg	40	Greenberg	183*	Gehringer	.371*
1938	Fox	186	Greenberg	58*	Greenberg	146	Greenberg	.315
1939	McCosky	190	Greenberg	33	Greenberg	112	Gehringer	.325
1940	McCosky	200†	Greenberg	41*	Greenberg	150*	Greenberg	.340
1941	Higgins	161	York	27	York	111	McCosky	.324
1942	McCosky	176	York	21	York	90	McCosky	.293
1943	Wakefield	200*	York	34*	York	118*	Wakefield	.316
1944	Cramer	169	York	18	York	98	Higgins	.297
1945	York	157	Cullenbine	18	Cullenbine	93	Mayo	.285
			York	18				
1946	Lake	149	Greenberg	44*	Greenberg	127*	Kell	.327
1947	Kell	188	Cullenbine	24	Kell	93	Kell	.320
1948	Evers	169	Mullin	23	Evers	103	Evers	.314
1949	Wertz	185	Wertz	20	Wertz	133	Kell	.343*
1950	Kell	218*	Wertz	27	Wertz	123	Kell	.340
1951	Kell	191*	Wertz	27	Wertz	94	Kell	.319
1952	Groth	149	Dropo	23	Dropo	70	Groth	.284
1953	Kuenn	209*	Boone	22	Dropo	96	Kuenn	.308
1954	Kuenn	201†	Boone	20	Boone	85	Kuenn	.306
1955	Kaline	200*	Kaline	27	Boone	116†	Kaline	.340*
1956	Kuenn	196*	Maxwell	28	Kaline	128	Kuenn	.332
1957	Kuenn	173	Maxwell	24	Kaline	90	Kaline	.295
1958	Kuenn	179	Harris	20	Kaline	85	Kuenn	.319
1959	Kuenn	198*	Maxwell	31	Maxwell	95	Kuenn	.353*
1960	Kaline	153	Colavito	35	Colavito	87	Kaline	.278
1961	Cash	193*	Colavito	45	Colavito	140	Cash	.361*
1962	Colavito	164	Cash	39	Colavito	112	Bruton	.278
1963	Kaline	172	Kaline	27	Kaline	101	Kaline	.312
1964	Lumpe	160	McAuliffe	24	Cash	83	Freehan	.300
1965	Wert	159	Cash	30	Horton	104	Horton	.273
1966	Cash	168	Cash	32	Horton	100	Kaline	.288
1967	Freehan	146	Kaline	25	Kaline	78	Kaline	.308
1968	Northrup	153	Horton	36	Northrup	90	Horton	.285
1969	Northrup	160	Horton	28	Horton	91	Northrup	.295
1970	Stanley	143	Northrup	24	Northrup	80	Kaline	.278

*Led league   †Tied for league lead

APPENDICES

Year	Leader in Hits		Leader in HR		Leader in RBI		Leader in AVG	
1971	Rodriguez	153	Cash	32	Cash	91	Kaline	.294
1972	Rodriguez	142	Cash	22	Cash	61	Northrup	.261
1973	Stanley	147	Cash	19	Rodriguez	58	Horton	.316
1974	Sutherland	157	Freehan	18	Kaline	64	Freehan	.297
1975	Horton	169	Horton	25	Horton	92	Horton	.275
1976	Staub	176	Thompson	17	Staub	96	LeFlore	.316
1977	LeFlore	212	Thompson	31	Thompson	105	LeFlore	.325
1978	LeFlore	198	Thompson	26	Staub	121	LeFlore	.297
1979	LeFlore	180	Kemp	26	Kemp	105	Kemp	.318
1980	Trammell	168	Parrish	24	Kemp	101	Trammell	.300
1981	Kemp	103	Parrish	10	Kemp	49	Gibson	.328
1982	Herndon	179	Parrish	32	Herndon	88	Herndon	.292
1983	Whitaker	206	Parrish	27	Parrish	114	Whitaker	.320
1984	Trammell	174	Parrish	33	Parrish	98	Trammell	.314
1985	Whitaker	170	Evans	40*	Parrish	98	Gibson	.287
1986	Trammell	159	Evans	29	Coles	86	Trammell	.277
					Gibson	86		
1987	Trammell	205	Evans	34	Trammell	105	Trammell	.343
1988	Trammell	145	Evans	22	Trammell	69	Trammell	.311

*Led league   †Tied for league lead

Tiger Career Batting Leaders
(Detroit records only, not including Post-Season)

GAMES

Kaline	2,834
Cobb	2,805
Gehringer	2,323
Crawford	2,114
Cash	2,018
Heilmann	1,989
Bush	1,872
Freehan	1,774
McAuliffe	1,656
Veach	1,605

AT BATS

Cobb	10,586
Kaline	10,116
Gehringer	8,860
Crawford	7,994
Heilmann	7,297
Bush	6,966
Cash	6,593
Freehan	6,073
Veach	5,982
McAuliffe	5,898

RUNS

Cobb	2,087
Gehringer	1,774
Kaline	1,622
Bush	1,242
Heilmann	1,209
Crawford	1,115
Cash	1,028
Greenberg	980
Trammell	884
Veach	859
McAuliffe	856

DOUBLES

Cobb	665
Gehringer	574
Kaline	498
Heilmann	497
Crawford	403
Greenberg	366
Veach	345
Trammell	272
Kuenn	244
Cash	241
Freehan	241

TRIPLES

Cobb	286
Crawford	250
Gehringer	146
Heilmann	145
Veach	136
Kaline	75
Bush	73
McAuliffe	70
Greenberg	69
Blue	66

HOME RUNS

Kaline	399
Cash	373
Greenberg	306
Horton	262
York	239
Parrish	212
Freehan	200
McAuliffe	192
Gehringer	184
Heilmann	164

RBI

Cobb	1,828
Kaline	1,583
Heilmann	1,454
Gehringer	1,427
Crawford	1,264
Greenberg	1,202
Cash	1,087
Veach	1,042
York	936
Horton	886

EXTRA-BASE HITS

Cobb	1,063
Kaline	972
Gehringer	904
Heilmann	806
Greenberg	741
Crawford	723
Cash	654
Veach	540
York	517
Horton	504

TOTAL BASES

Cobb	5,475
Kaline	4,852
Gehringer	4,257
Heilmann	3,778
Crawford	3,579
Cash	3,233
Greenberg	2,950
Veach	2,654
Horton	2,549
Freehan	2,502

HITS

Cobb	3,902
Kaline	3,007
Gehringer	2,839
Heilmann	2,499
Crawford	2,466
Veach	1,860
Cash	1,793
Bush	1,744
Freehan	1,591
Trammell	1,550
Greenberg	1,528

BATTING

Cobb	369
Heilmann	342
Fothergill	337
Kell	325
Manush	321
Gehringer	320
Greenberg	319
G. Walker	317
Kuenn	314
McCosky	312

STOLEN BASES

Cobb	865
Bush	400
Crawford	317
LeFlore	294
Moriarty	190
Veach	189
Gehringer	182
Trammell	177
Gibson	166
Jones	140

Pitching Leaders by Year

Year	Leader in Wins		Leader in Losses		Leader in IP		Leader in ERA	
1901	Miller	23	Cronin	15	Miller	332	Yeager	2.61
			Siever	15				
1902	Mercer	15	Mercer	18	Mercer	282	Siever	1.91*
1903	Mullin	19	Donovan	16	Mullin	321	Mullin	2.25
			Kitson	16				
1904	Donovan	17	Mullin	23	Mullin	382	Mullin	2.40
	Mullin	17						
1905	Killian	23	Mullin	21	Mullin	348*	Killian	2.27
1906	Mullin	21	Mullin	18	Mullin	330	Siever	2.71
1907	Donovan	25	Mullin	20	Mullin	357	Killian	1.78
	Killian	25						
1908	Summers	24	Mullin	13	Summers	301	Summers	1.64
1909	Mullin	29*	Willett	10	Mullin	304	Killian	1.71
1910	Mullin	21	Mullin	12	Mullin	289	Donovan	2.42
			Summers	12				
1911	Mullin	18	Willett	14	Mullin	234	Mullin	3.07
1912	Dubuc	17	Mullin	17	Willett	284	Dubuc	2.77
	Willett	17						
1913	Dubuc	15	Dubuc	14	Dubuc	243	Dauss	2.68
			Willett	14				
1914	Coveleski	21	Dauss	15	Coveleski	303	Coveleski	2.49
1915	Dauss	24	Coveleski	13	Coveleski	313	Coveleski	2.45
			Dauss	13				
1916	Coveleski	21	Dauss	12	Coveleski	324	Coveleski	1.97
			James	12				
1917	Dauss	17	Ehmke	15	Dauss	271	James	2.09
1918	Boland	14	Dauss	16	Dauss	250	Boland	2.65
1919	Dauss	21	Boland	16	Dauss	256	Leonard	2.77
1920	Ehmke	15	Dauss	21	Dauss	270	Ehmke	3.29
1921	Ehmke	13	Dauss	15	Leonard	245	Leonard	3.75
1922	Pillette	19	Ehmke	17	Ehmke	280	Pillette	2.85
1923	Dauss	21	Pillette	19†	Dauss	316	Dauss	3.62
1924	Whitehill	17	Dauss	11	Whitehill	233	Collins	3.21
			Stoner	11				
1925	Dauss	16	Collins	11	Whitehill	239	Dauss	3.16
			Dauss	11				
			Whitehill	11				
1926	Whitehill	16	Whitehill	13	Whitehill	252	Gibson	3.48
1927	Whitehill	16	Whitehill	14	Whitehill	236	Whitehill	3.36
1928	Carroll	16	Whitehill	16	Carroll	231	Carroll	3.27

*Led league   †Tied for league lead

Year	Leader in Wins		Leader in Losses		Leader in IP		Leader in ERA	
1929	Uhle	15	Carroll	17	Uhle	249	Uhle	4.08
1930	Whitehill	17	Whitehill	13	Uhle	239	Uhle	3.65
1931	Sorrell	13	Bridges	16	Whitehill	272	Uhle	3.50
	Whitehill	13	Whitehill	16				
1932	Whitehill	16	Sorrell	14	Whitehill	244	Bridges	3.36
1933	Marberry	16	Fischer	15	Marberry	238	Bridges	3.09
			Sorrell	15				
1934	Rowe	24	Bridges	11	Bridges	275	Auker	3.42
1935	Bridges	21	Rowe	13	Rowe	276	Bridges	3.51
1936	Bridges	23*	Auker	16	Bridges	295	Bridges	3.60
1937	Lawson	18	Bridges	12	Auker	253	Auker	3.88
1938	Bridges	13	Auker	10	Kennedy	190	Gill	4.12
1939	Bridges	17	Rowe	12	Newsom	246	Newsom	3.37
	Newsom	17						
1940	Newsom	21	Benton	10	Newsom	264	Newsom	2.83
1941	Benton	15	Newsom	20*	Newsom	250	Benton	2.97
1942	Trucks	14	Trout	18	Benton	227	Newhouser	2.45
1943	Trout	20†	Newhouser	17	Trout	247	Bridges	2.39
1944	Newhouser	29*	Gentry	14	Trout	352*	Trout	2.12
			Gorsica	14				
			Trout	14				
1945	Newhouser	25*	Trout	15	Newhouser	313	Newhouser	1.81
1946	Newhouser	26†	Trout	13	Newhouser	292	Newhouser	1.94
1947	Hutchinson	18	Newhouser	17*	Newhouser	285	Newhouser	2.87
1948	Newhouser	21*	Houtteman	16	Newhouser	272	Newhouser	3.01
1949	Trucks	19	Newhouser	11	Newhouser	292	Trucks	2.81
			Trucks	11				
1950	Houtteman	19	Newhouser	13	Houtteman	275	Houtteman	3.54
1951	Trucks	13	Gray	14†	Gray	197	Hutchinson	3.68
			Trout	14†				
1952	Gray	12	Houtteman	20*	Gray	224	Newhouser	3.74
1953	Garver	11	Gray	15	Garver	198	Garver	4.45
1954	Gromek	18	Gromek	16	Gromek	253*	Gromek	2.74
1955	Hoeft	16	Garver	16	Lary	235	Hoeft	2.99
1956	Lary	21*	Hoeft	14	Lary	294*	Lary	3.15
1957	Bunning	20†	Lary	16	Bunning	267*	Bunning	2.69
1958	Lary	16	Lary	15	Lary	260*	Lary	2.90
1959	Bunning	17	Foytack	14	Bunning	250	Mossi	3.36
	Lary	17						
	Mossi	17						
1960	Lary	15	Lary	15	Lary	274*	Bunning	2.79
1961	Lary	23	Bunning	11	Lary	275	Mossi	2.96
1962	Bunning	19	Mossi	13	Bunning	258	Aguirre	2.21*

*Led league   †Tied for league lead

Year	Leader in Wins		Leader in Losses		Leader in IP		Leader in ERA	
1963	Regan	15	Aguirre	15	Bunning	248	Aguirre	3.67
1964	Wickersham	19	Wickersham	12	Wickersham	254	Lolich	3.26
1965	McLain	16	Wickersham	14	Lolich	244	McLain	2.61
1966	McLain	20	Lolich	14	McLain	264	Wilson	2.59
			McLain	14				
1967	Wilson	22	McLain	16	Wilson	264	Lolich	3.04
1968	McLain	31*	Wilson	12	McLain	336*	McLain	1.96
1969	McLain	24*	Lolich	11	McLain	325*	McLain	2.80
1970	Lolich	14	Lolich	19*	Lolich	273	Lolich	3.79
1971	Lolich	25*	Lolich	14	Lolich	376*	Lolich	2.92
1972	Lolich	22	Coleman	14	Lolich	327	Lolich	2.50
			Lolich	14				
1973	Coleman	23	Coleman	15	Lolich	309	Coleman	3.53
			Lolich	15				
1974	Hiller	17	Lolich	21*	Lolich	308	Lolich	4.15
1975	Lolich	12	Coleman	18	Lolich	241	Lolich	3.78
			Lolich	18				
1976	Fidrych	19	Roberts	17	Roberts	252	Fidrych	2.34*
1977	Rozema	15	Arroyo	18	Rozema	218	Rozema	3.09
1978	Slaton	17	Rozema	12	Slaton	234	Rozema	3.14
			Wilcox	12				
1979	Morris	17	Wilcox	10	Morris	198	Morris	3.28
1980	Morris	16	Morris	15	Morris	250	Petry	3.94
1981	Morris	14†	Petry	9	Morris	198	Petry	3.00
			Wilcox	9				
1982	Morris	17	Morris	16	Morris	266	Petry	3.22
1983	Morris	20	Morris	13	Morris	294*	Morris	3.34
1984	Morris	19	Morris	11	Morris	241	Petry	3.24
1985	Morris	16	Petry	13	Morris	257	Morris	3.33
1986	Morris	21	Terrell	12	Morris	267	Morris	3.27
1987	Morris	18	Morris	11	Morris	266	Morris	3.38
1988	Morris	15	Terrell	16	Morris	235	Morris	3.94

*Led league   †Tied for league lead

Tiger Career Pitching Leaders
(Detroit records only, not including Post-Season)

GAMES

Hiller	545
Dauss	538
Lolich	508
Trout	493
Newhouser	460
Mullin	435
Bridges	424
Morris	370
Lopez	355
Aguirre	334

GAMES STARTED

Lolich	459
Mullin	395
Dauss	388
Newhouser	373
Bridges	362
Morris	348
Trout	305
Whitehill	287
Lary	274
Bunning	251

STRIKEOUTS

Lolich	2,679
Newhouser	1,770
Morris	1,703
Bridges	1,674
Bunning	1,406
Mullin	1,380
Dauss	1,201
Trout	1,199
McLain	1,150
Donovan	1,079

GAMES WON

Dauss	221
Mullin	209
Lolich	207
Newhouser	200
Bridges	194
Morris	177
Trout	161
Donovan	141
Whitehill	133
Lary	123

COMPLETE GAMES

Mullin	336
Dauss	245
Donovan	213
Newhouser	212
Bridges	207
Lolich	190
Trout	156
Whitehill	148
Killian	142
Morris	133
Willett	127
Lary	123

SAVES

Hiller	125
Hernandez	105
Lopez	85
Fox	55
Benton	45
Dauss	39
Sherry	37
Scherman	34
Trout	34
Gladding	33
Timmerman	33

GAMES LOST

Dauss	183
Mullin	179
Lolich	175
Trout	153
Newhouser	148
Bridges	138
Whitehill	119
Morris	118
Lary	110

INNINGS PITCHED

Mullin	3,394
Dauss	3,391
Lolich	3,362
Newhouser	2,944
Bridges	2,826
Morris	2,624
Trout	2,592
Whitehill	2,172
Donovan	2,139
Lary	2,009

SHUTOUTS

Lolich	39
Mullin	34
Bridges	33
Newhouser	33
Donovan	29
Trout	28
McLain	26
Dauss	22
Trucks	22

20-WIN SEASONS

Mullin	5
Newhouser	4
Bridges	3
Coveleski	3
Dauss	3
McLain	3

Tigers to Remember

Batting Champions

1907	Ty Cobb	.350	1919	Ty Cobb	.384
1908	Ty Cobb	.324	1921	Harry Heilmann	.394
1909	Ty Cobb	.377	1923	Harry Heilmann	.403
1910	Ty Cobb	.385	1925	Harry Heilmann	.393
1911	Ty Cobb	.420	1926	Heinie Manush	.378
1912	Ty Cobb	.410	1927	Harry Heilmann	.398
1913	Ty Cobb	.390	1937	Charlie Gehringer	.371
1914	Ty Cobb	.368	1949	George Kell	.343
1915	Ty Cobb	.369	1955	Al Kaline	.340
1917	Ty Cobb	.383	1959	Harvey Kuenn	.353
1918	Ty Cobb	.382	1961	Norm Cash	.361

Home Run Champions

1908	Sam Crawford	7	1940	Hank Greenberg	41
1909	Ty Cobb	9	1943	Rudy York	34
1935	Hank Greenberg	36†	1946	Hank Greenberg	44
1938	Hank Greenberg	58	1985	Darrell Evans	40

RBI Champions

1907	Ty Cobb	116	1917	Bobby Veach	103
1908	Ty Cobb	108	1918	Bobby Veach	78
1909	Ty Cobb	107	1935	Hank Greenberg	170
1910	Sam Crawford	120	1937	Hank Greenberg	183
1911	Ty Cobb	144	1940	Hank Greenberg	150
1914	Sam Crawford	104	1943	Rudy York	118
1915	Sam Crawford	112†	1946	Hank Greenberg	127
1914	Bobby Veach	112†	1955	Ray Boone	116†

†Tied for league lead

Triple Crown Winner

1909   Ty Cobb (Batted .377 with 9 home runs and 107 RBI). Also led league with 216 hits, .517 slugging percentage, 296 total bases, 76 stolen bases and 116 runs scored.

Baseball Writers Association of America Awards

Chalmers Award (AL)
1911   Ty Cobb

Most Valuable Player (AL)
1934   Mickey Cochrane
1935   Hank Greenberg
1937   Charlie Gehringer
1940   Hank Greenberg
1944   Hal Newhouser
1945   Hal Newhouser
1968   Denny McLain
1984   Willie Hernandez

Cy Young Award (AL)
1968   Denny McLain (unanimous)
1969   Denny McLain (tied)
1984   Willie Hernandez

Rookie of the Year (AL)
1953   Harvey Kuenn
1976   Mark Fidrych
1978   Lou Whitaker

Manager of the Year (AL)
1984   Sparky Anderson
1987   Sparky Anderson

Gold Glove Awards

1957 Al Kaline, of	1966 Bill Freehan, c	1976 Aurelio Rodriguez, 3b
1948 Frank Bolling, 2b	Al Kaline, of	1980 Alan Trammell, ss
Al Kaline, of	1967 Bill Freehan, c	1981 Alan Trammell, ss
1959 Al Kaline, of	Al Kaline, of	1983 Lance Parrish, c
1961 Al Kaline, of	1968 Bill Freehan, c	Alan Trammell, ss
Frank Lary, p	Mickey Stanley, of	Lou Whitaker, 2b
1962 Al Kaline, of	1969 Bill Freehan, c	1984 Lance Parrish, c
1963 Al Kaline, of	Mickey Stanley, of	Alan Trammell, ss
1964 Al Kaline, of	1970 Mickey Stanley, of	Lou Whitaker 2b
1965 Bill Freehan, c	1972 Ed Brinkman, ss	1985 Lance Parrish, c
Al Kaline, of	1973 Mickey Stanley, of	Lou Whitaker, 2b
		1988 Gary Pettis, of

Tiger of the Year
(Selected by Detroit Baseball Writers Assn.)

1965—Don Wert	1973—John Hiller	1981—Kirk Gibson
1966—Denny McLain	1974—Al Kaline	1982—Lance Parrish
1967—Bill Freehan	1975—Willie Horton	1983—Lou Whitaker
1968—Denny McLain	1976—Mark Fidrych	1984—Willie Hernandez
1969—Denny McLain	1977—Ron LeFlore	1985—Darrell Evans
1970—Tom Timmerman	1978—Ron LeFlore	1986—Jack Morris
1971—Mickey Lolich	1979—Steve Kemp	1987—Alan Trammell
1972—Ed Brinkman	1980—Alan Trammell	1988—Alan Trammell

Rookie of the Year
(Selected by Detroit Sports Broadcasters Assn.)

1969—Mike Kilkenny	1975—Vern Ruhle	1982—Glenn Wilson
1970—Elliott Maddox	1976—Mark Fidrych	1983—Dave Gumpert
1971—None awarded	1977—Dave Rozema	1984—Barbaro Garbey
1972—Chuck Seelbach	1978—Lou Whitaker	1985—Nelson Simmons
1973—Dick Sharon	1979—Lynn Jones	1986—Eric King
1974—Ron LeFlore	1980—Rick Peters	1987—Matt Nokes
	1981—None awarded	1988—Paul Gibson

Other Awards

Roberto Clemente Award
1973   Al Kaline

Joseph E. Cronin Trophy
1974   Al Kaline

Loy Gehrig Trophy
1970   Al Kaline

Thr Hutch Award
1970   Al Kaline
1973   John Hiller

Comeback Player of the Year (AL)
1965   Norm Cash
1971   Norm Cash
1973   John Hiller
1983   Alan Trammell

Designated Hitter of the Year
1975   Willie Horton
1978   Rusty Staub

ALCS Most Valuable Player
1984   Kirk Gibson

World Series Most Valuable Player
1968   Mickey Lolich
1984   Alan Trammell

American League
Player/Pitcher of the Month
1974   Al Kaline . . . . September
1976   Willie Horton . . . . April
        Ron LeFlore . . . . May
        Mark Fidrych . . . . June
1983   Jack Morris . . . . August
1984   Jack Morris . . . . April
        Alan Trammell . . . . April
        Willie Hernandez . . . . . . June
1987   Doyle Alexander . September
        Alan Trammell . . September

American League
Player of the Week
1975   Willie Horton . . . . Aug 3
1976   Willie Horton . . . . April 25
        Ron LeFlore . . . . May 9
        Ben Oglivie . . . . June 6
1978   Jason Thompson . . June 25
1979   Lance Parrish . . . . . . May 29
1980   Alan Trammell . . . . . May 12
        Tom Brookens . . . . . . Aug 18
        Steve Kemp . . . . Sept 14
1981   Kirk Gibson . . . . Aug 24
        Kirk Gibson . . . . Sept 28
1982   Larry Herndon . . . . . May 17
1983   Milt Wilcox . . . . April 11
        Lou Whitaker . . . . June 6
1984   Jack Morris . . . . April 2
        Lance Parrish . . . . . June 18
1985   Darrell Evans . . . . . . May 13
        Kirk Gibson . . . . June 3
        Darrell Evans . . . . . . Sept 16
1986   Kirk Gibson . . . . April 7
        Kirk Gibson . . . . June 23
        Jack Morris . . . . July 7
        Kirk Gibson . . . . July 14
        John Grubb . . . . July 21
        Jack Morris . . . . Sept 22

AP All Star Team
1988   Alan Trammell

National Baseball Hall of Fame

	Pos.	Year Selected	Years at Detroit	Playing Career
Averill, Earl	of	1975	1939-40	1929-41
Barrow, Edward G.	mgr	1953	1903-04	
Brouthers, Dan	1b	1945	1886-88*	1879-1904
Cobb, Ty	of-mgr	1936	1905-26	1905-28
Cochrane, Mickey	c-mgr	1947	1934-38	1925-37
Crawford, Sam	of	1957	1903-17	1899-1917
Evans, Billy	gen mgr	1973	1947-51	
Ferrell, Rick	gen mgr-scout	1984	1950-	1929-47
Gehringer, Charlie	if	1949	1924-42	1924-42
Goslin, Goose	of	1968	1934-37	1921-38
Greenberg, Hank	1b-of	1956	1930-46	1930-47
Harris, Bucky	if-mgr	1975	1929-33 1955-56	1919-31
Heilmann, Harry	of-1b	1952	1914-29	1914-32
Hoyt, Waite	p	1969	1930-31	1918-38
Jennings, Hughie	ss-mgr	1945	1907-20	1891-1918
Kaline, Al	of	1980	1953-74	1953-74
Kell, George	if	1983	1946-52	1943-57
Manush, Heinie	of	1964	1923-27	1923-39
Mathews, Eddie	3b-1b	1978	1967-68	1952-68
Simmons, Al	of	1953	1936	1924-44
Thompson, Sam	of	1974	1885-88* 1906	1885-1906

*Detroit in National League

Tiger All-Star Game Selections

1988
Doyle Alexander
Alan Trammell

1987
Jack Morris
Matt Nokes
Alan Trammell

1986
Willie Hernandez
Lance Parrish*
Lou Whitaker*

1985
Willie Hernandez
Jack Morris*
Lance Parrish*‡
Dan Petry
Alan Trammell
Lou Whitaker*

1984
Willie Hernandez
Chet Lemon*
Jack Morris
Lance Parrish*
Alan Trammell‡
Lou Whitaker*

1983
Aurelio Lopez
Lance Parrish
Lou Whitaker

1982
Lance Parrish

1981
Jack Morris*

1980
Lance Parrish
Alan Trammell

1979
Steve Kemp

1978
Jason Thompson

1977
Mark Fidrych‡
Jason Thompson

1976
Mark Fidrych*
Ron LeFlore*
Rusty Staub*

*Voted starter or started   ‡Selected but unable to play.   †Two games 1959–62.

1975

Bill Freehan

1974

John Hiller
Al Kaline

1973

Ed Brinkman
Bill Freehan
Willie Horton

1972

Norm Cash
Bill Freehan*
Mickey Lolich

1971

Norm Cash*
Bill Freehan*
Al Kaline
Mickey Lolich

1970

Bill Freehan*
Willie Horton

1969

Bill Freehan*
Mickey Lolich
Denny McLain

1968

Bill Freehan*
Willie Horton*
Denny McLain
Don Wert

1967

Bill Freehan*
Al Kaline*
Dick McAuliffe

1966

Norm Cash
Bill Freehan*
Al Kaline
Dick McAuliffe*
Denny McLain*

1965

Bill Freehan
Willie Horton*
Al Kaline
Dick McAuliffe*

1964

Bill Freehan
Al Kaline
Jerry Lumpe

1963

Jim Bunning
Al Kaline*

1962

Hank Aguirre†
Jim Bunning†
Rocky Colavito†
Al Kaline

1961

Jim Bunning†
Norm Cash*†
Al Kaline†
Frank Lary

1960

Al Kaline†
Frank Lary†

1959

Jim Bunning
Al Kaline†
Harvey Kuenn†

1958

Al Kaline
Harvey Kuenn

1957

Jim Bunning*
Al Kaline*
Harvey Kuenn*
Charley Maxwell

1956

Ray Bonne
Al Kaline*
Harvey Kuenn*
Charley Maxwell

1955

Billy Hoeft
Al Kaline*
Harvey Kuenn*

1954

Ray Boone*
Harvey Kuenn

1953

Harvey Kuenn

1952

Vic Wertz

1951

Fred Hutchinson
George Kell*
Vic Wertz*

1950

Hoot Evers*
Ted Gray
Art Houtteman
George Kell*

1949

George Kell*
Virgil Trucks
Vic Wertz

1948

Hoot Evers*
George Kell*
Pat Mullin*
Hal Newhouser

1947

George Kell*
Pat Mullin
Hal Newhouser*
Dizzy Trout

1946

Hal Newhouser

1945

No game

1944

Pinky Higgins
Hal Newhouser
Dizzy Trout
Rudy York

1943

Hal Newhouser
Dick Wakefield*
Rudy York

1942

Al Benton
Hal Newhouser
Birdie Tebbetts*
Rudy York*

1941

Al Benton
Birdie Tebbetts*
Rudy York*

1940

Tommy Bridges
Hank Greenberg*
Bobo Newsom

1939

Tommy Bridges*
Hank Greenberg*
Bobo Newsom

1938

Charlie Gehringer*
Hank Greenberg
Vern Kennedy
Rudy York

1937

Tommy Bridges
Charlie Gehringer*
Hank Greenberg
Gerald Walker

1936

Tommy Bridges
Charlie Gehringer*
Leon Goslin
Schoolboy Rowe

1935

Tommy Bridges
Mickey Cochrane
Charlie Gehringer*
Schoolboy Rowe

1934

Tommy Bridges
Mickey Cochrane
Charlie Gehringer*

1933

Charlie Gehringer*

Tigers Selected to the Most All-Star Games

18—Kaline, 1955-56-57-58-59*-
60*-61*-62-63-64-
65-66-67-71-74

11—Freehan, 1964-65-66-67-
68-69-70-71-72-
73-75

8—Kuenn, 1953-54-55-56-57-
58-59*

7—Bunning, 1957-59-61*-
62*-63

6—Bridges, 1934-35-36-37-
38-40
Gehringer, 1933-34-35-36-
37-38
Newhouser, 1942-43-44-
46-47-48
Parrish, 1980-82-83-84-85-
86

5—Cash, 1961*-66-71-72
Kell, 1947-48-49-50-51
Trammell, 1980-84-85-87-
88
York, 1938-41-42-43-44

4—Colavito, 1961*-62*
Greenberg, 1937-38-39-40
Horton, 1965-68-70-73
Morris, 1981-84-85-87
Whitaker, 1983-84-85-86

3—Hernandez, 1984-85-86
Lary, 1960*-61
Lolich, 1969-71-72
McLain, 1966-68-69
Wertz, 1949-51-52

*Two games

Detroit in American League

Year	Pos.	W-L	Pct	GA GB	Manager	Attendance
1968	**1**	**103-59**	**.636**	**12**	**Mayo Smith**	**2,031,847**
1967	T2	91-71	.562	1	Mayo Smith	1,447,143
1966	3	88-74	.543	10	Dressen-Swift*-Frank Skaff*	1,124,293
1965	4	89-73	.549	13	Chuck Dressen-Bob Swift*	1,029,645
1964	4	85-77	.525	14	Chuck Dressen	816,139
1963	T5	79-83	.488	25½	Bob Scheffing-Chuck Dressen	821,952
1962	4	85-76	.528	10½	Bob Scheffing	1,207,881
1961	2	101-61	.623	8	Bob Scheffing	1,600,710
1960	6	71-83	.461	26	Jimmie Dykes-Joe Gordon	1,167,669
1959	4	76-78	.494	18	Bill Norman-Jimmie Dykes	1,221,221
1958	5	77-77	.500	15	Jack Tighe-Bill Norman*	1,098,924
1957	4	78-76	.506	20	Jack Tighe	1,272,346
1956	5	82-72	.532	15	Bucky Harris	1,051,182
1955	5	79-75	.513	17	Bucky Harris	1,181,838
1954	5	68-86	.442	43	Fred Hutchinson	1,079,847
1953	6	60-94	.390	40½	Fred Hutchinson	884,658
1952	8	50-104	.325	45	Red Rolfe-Fred Hutchinson	1,026,846
1951	5	73-81	.474	25	Red Rolfe	1,132,641

Year	Pos.	W-L	Pct	GA GB	Manager	Attendance
1950	2	95-59	.617	3	Red Rolfe	1,951,474
1949	4	87-67	.565	10	Red Rolfe	1,821,204
1948	5	78-76	.506	18½	Steve O'Neill	1,743,035
1947	2	85-69	.552	12	Steve O'Neill	1,398,093
1946	2	92-62	.597	12	Steve O'Neill	1,722,590
1945	**1**	**88-65**	**.575**	**1½**	**Steve O'Neill**	**1,280,341**
1944	2	88-66	.571	1	Steve O'Neill	923,176
1943	5	78-76	.506	20	Steve O'Neill	606,287
1942	5	73-81	.474	30	Del Baker	580,087
1941	T4	75-79	.487	26	Del Baker	684,915
1940	**1**	**90-64**	**.584**	**1**	**Del Baker**	**1,112,693**
1939	5	81-73	.526	26½	Del Baker	836,279
1938	4	84-70	.545	16	Mickey Cochrane-Del Baker	799,557
1937	2	89-65	.578	13	Mickey Cochrane	1,072,276
1936	2	83-71	.539	19½	Mickey Cochrane	875,948
1935	**1**	**93-58**	**.616**	**3**	**Mickey Cochrane**	**1,034,929**
1934	**1**	**101-53**	**.656**	**7**	**Mickey Cochrane**	**919,161**
1933	5	75-79	.487	25	Bucky Harris-Del Baker*	320,972
1932	5	76-75	.503	29½	Bucky Harris	397,157
1931	7	61-93	.396	47	Bucky Harris	453,056
1930	5	75-79	.487	27	Bucky Harris	649,450
1929	6	70-84	.455	36	Bucky Harris	869,318
1928	6	68-86	.442	33	George Moriarty	474,323
1927	4	82-71	.536	27½	George Moriarty	773,716
1926	6	79-75	.513	12	Ty Cobb	711,914
1925	4	81-73	.526	16½	Ty Cobb	820,766
1924	3	86-68	.558	6	Ty Cobb	1,015,136
1923	2	83-71	.539	16	Ty Cobb	911,377
1922	3	79-75	.513	15	Ty Cobb	861,206
1921	6	71-82	.464	27	Ty Cobb	661,527
1920	7	61-93	.396	37	Hughie Jennings	579,650
1919	4	80-60	.571	8	Hughie Jennings	643,805
1918	7	55-71	.437	20	Hughie Jennings	203,719
1917	4	78-75	.510	21½	Hughie Jennings	457,289
1916	3	87-67	.565	4	Hughie Jennings	616,772
1915	2	100-54	.649	2½	Hughie Jennings	476,105
1914	4	80-73	.523	19½	Hughie Jennings	416,225
1913	6	66-87	.431	30	Hughie Jennings	398,502
1912	6	69-84	.451	36½	Hughie Jennings	402,870
1911	2	89-65	.578	13½	Hughie Jennings	484,988
1910	3	86-68	.558	18	Hughie Jennings	391,288
1909	**1**	**98-54**	**.645**	**3½**	**Hughie Jennings**	**490,490**
1908	**1**	**90-63**	**.588**	**½**	**Hughie Jennings**	**436,199**
1907	**1**	**92-58**	**.613**	**1½**	**Hughie Jennings**	**297,079**

Year	Pos.	W-L	Pct	GA GB	Manager	Attendance
1906	6	71-78	.477	21	Bill Armour	174,043
1905	3	79-74	.516	15½	Bill Armour	193,384
1904	7	62-90	.408	32	Ed Barrow-Bobby Lowe*	177,796
1903	5	65-71	.478	25	Ed Barrow	224,523
1902	7	52-83	.385	30½	Frank Dwyer	189,469
1901	3	74-61	.548	8½	George Stallings	259,430

Tigers in National League

Detroit was member of National League from 1881 through 1888, dropped out of majors until 1901, to return as charter member of American League.

Tigers of 1887 won National League pennant by 3½ games, engaged St. Louis champions of American Association in 15-game post-season series which was forerunner of World Series. Detroit won 10 of 15 games in cross-country tour.

Year	Pos.	W-L	Pct	GA GB	Manager
1881	4	41-43	.488	15	Frank Bancroft
1882	6	42-41	.506	12½	Frank Bancroft
1883	7	40-58	.408	23	Jack Chapman
1884	8	28-84	.250	56	Jack Chapman
1885	6	41-67	.380	44	Charlie Morton-Bill Watkins
1886	2	87-36	.707	2½	Bill Watkins
1887	**1**	**79-45**	**.637**	**3½**	**Bill Watkins**
1888	5	68-63	.519	16	Bill Watkins-Bob Leadly

Detroit in AL East Division

Year	Pos.	W-L	Pct	GA GB	Manager	Attendance
1988	2	88-74	.543	1	Sparky Anderson	2,081,162
1987	**1**	**98-64**	**.605**	**2**	**Sparky Anderson**	**2,061,829**
1986	3	87-75	.537	8½	Sparky Anderson	1,899,437
1985	3	84-77	.522	15	Sparky Anderson	2,286,609
1984	**1**	**104-58**	**.642**	**15**	**Sparky Anderson**	**2,704,794**
1983	2	92-70	.568	6	Sparky Anderson	1,829,636
1982	4	83-79	.512	12	Sparky Anderson	1,636,058
1981	4	60-49	.550	2	Sparky Anderson	1,149,144
	T2	29-23	.558	1½	(2nd Half)	
	4	31-26	.544	3½	(1st Half)	
1980	5	84-78	.519	19	Sparky Anderson	1,785,293
1979	5	85-76	.528	18	Les Moss-Sparky Anderson	1,630,929
1978	5	86-76	.531	13½	Ralph Houk	1,714,893
1977	4	74-88	.457	26	Ralph Houk	1,359,856
1976	5	74-87	.460	24	Ralph Houk	1,467,020
1975	6	57-102	.358	37½	Ralph Houk	1,058,836
1974	6	72-90	.444	19	Ralph Houk	1,243,080
1973	3	85-77	.525	12	Billy Martin-Joe Schultz*	1,724,146
1972	**1**	**86-70**	**.551**	**½**	**Billy Martin**	**1,892,386**
1971	2	91-71	.562	12	Billy Martin	1,591,073
1970	4	79-83	.488	29	Mayo Smith	1,501,293
1969	2	90-72	.556	19	Mayo Smith	1,577,481
TOTALS		**6986-6436**	**.520**		*Interim	**89,087,164**

First Night Game, June 15, 1948

Athletics

	*B.av.	Ab.	r.	h.	rbi.	sh.	sb.	o.	a.	e.
Joost, ss	.259	2	1	1	0	0	0	3	3	0
R. Coleman, rf	.227	3	0	0	0	0	0	1	0	0
McCosky, lf	.265	3	0	0	0	1	0	2	1	0
White, lf	.213	0	0	0	0	0	0	0	0	0
Fain, 1b	.253	3	0	0	0	0	0	6	0	0
Majeski, 3b	.295	4	0	1	1	0	0	2	2	0
Chapman, cf	.259	4	0	0	0	0	0	6	0	0
Rosar, c	.216	3	0	0	0	0	0	4	0	0
Suder, 2b	.253	2	0	0	0	0	0	0	1	0
J. Col'n, p (W7-L3)		3	0	0	0	0	0	0	1	0
Totals		27	1	2	1	1	0	24	8	0

Detroit Tigers

	*B.av.	Ab.	r.	h.	rbi.	sh.	sb.	o.	a.	e.
Lipon, ss	.287	4	0	0	0	0	0	2	3	0
Lake, 2b	.270	3	1	0	0	0	0	1	1	0
Kell, 3b	.346	3	1	1	0	0	0	4	2	0
Wakefield, lf	.299	3	1	1	1	0	0	1	0	0
Evers, cf	.318	3	0	2	2	0	0	4	0	0
Mullin, rf	.330	4	1	1	1	0	0	1	0	0
Vico, 1b	.269	4	0	2	0	0	0	9	1	0
Swift, c	.216	4	0	0	0	0	0	3	0	0
New'ser p (W8-L4)		2	0	0	0	0	0	0	1	0
Totals		30	4	7	4	0	0	27	8	0

Athletics _____ 1 0 0 0 0 0 0 0 0 __1

Detroit _____ 0 0 2 0 0 0 0 2 x __4

Trucks's First No Hitter, May 15, 1952

Washington	ab	r	h	o	a		Detroit	ab	r	h	o	a
Yost, 3b	3	0	0	2	1		Lipon, s	4	0	0	1	4
Busby, cf	3	0	0	3	0		Kell, 3b	3	0	1	1	2
Jensen, rf	4	0	0	2	0		Mullin, lf	4	0	0	3	0
Vernon, 1b	4	0	0	9	0		Wertz, rf	3	1	2	1	0
Runnels, ss	3	0	0	3	3		So'hock, 1b	3	0	0	9	0
Coan, lf	3	0	0	2	0		Ginsberg, c	3	0	0	7	0
Marsh, 2b	3	0	0	1	2		Groth, cf	3	0	0	5	0
Kluttz, c	2	0	0	4	2		Priddy, 2b	3	0	0	0	1
Por'field, p	3	0	0	0	0		Trucks, p	3	0	1	0	0
Totals	28	0	0x	26	8		Totals	29	1	4	27	7

x-Two out when winning run scored.

Washington ———————— 0 0 0 0 0 0 0 0 0—1
Detroit ———————— 0 0 0 0 0 0 0 0 1—1

Trucks's Second No Hitter, August 25, 1952

Detroit	ab	r	h	o	a		New York	ab	r	h	o	a
Groth, cf	4	0	0	2	0		Mantle, cf	3	0	0	3	0
Pesky, ss	4	0	0	3	2		Collins, 1b	4	0	0	10	1
Hatfield, 3b	3	0	1	2	0		Bauer, rf	4	0	0	0	1
Dropo, 1b	4	1	2	5	3		Berra, c	3	0	0	7	0
Scuch'k, rf	4	0	1	3	0		Woodling, lf	3	0	0	3	0
Delsing, lf	4	0	0	2	1		Babe, 3b	3	0	0	3	2
Batts, c	2	0	1	6	2		Martin, 2b	3	0	0	1	4
Federoff, 2b	3	0	0	0	1		Rizzuto, ss	2	0	0	0	5
Trucks, p	2	0	0	4	2		a-Mize	1	0	0	0	0
							Bridewe'r, ss	0	0	0	0	0
							Miller, p	1	0	0	0	1
							*b-Noren	1	0	0	0	0
							Scarbor'h, p	0	0	0	0	0
Totals	30	1	5	27	11		Totals	28	0	0	27	14

a-Fouled out for Rizzuto in 8th.
b-Flied out for Miller in 8th.

Detroit ———————— 0 0 0 0 0 0 1 0 0—1
New York ———————— 0 0 0 0 0 0 0 0 0—0

INDEX

◆